FROM DIGITAL BANKING TO AI FIRST BANKING

How Intelligence, Infrastructure, and Autonomy Will Redefine Financial Institutions

RAJ SINGH

AF721757

notionpress.com

INDIA • SINGAPORE • MALAYSIA

Copyright © Raj Singh 2026
All Rights Reserved.

ISBN

Paperback 979-8-90342-856-4
Hardcase 979-8-90510-354-4

This book has been published with all efforts made to make the material error-free after the consent of the author. However, the author and the publisher do not assume and hereby disclaim any liability to any party for any loss, damage, or disruption caused by errors or omissions, whether such errors or omissions result from negligence, accident, or any other cause.

While every effort has been made to avoid any mistake or omission, this publication is being sold on the condition and understanding that neither the author nor the publishers or printers would be liable in any manner to any person by reason of any mistake or omission in this publication or for any action taken or omitted to be taken or advice rendered or accepted on the basis of this work. For any defect in printing or binding the publishers will be liable only to replace the defective copy by another copy of this work then available.

Contents

Acknowledgement

No transformation is ever the work of one individual.

This book was written across continents, in boardrooms overlooking African skylines, in quiet hotel rooms between strategy sessions, in conversations with regulators, technologists, founders, and bankers who are wrestling with the same question:

What will banking become?

I have been privileged to stand inside institutions at moments of inflection, when legacy systems met digital ambition, when balance sheets met algorithms, when risk committees confronted machine intelligence for the first time. The ideas in this book were not born in isolation. They were shaped by dialogue, challenge, resistance, curiosity, and courage.

To the leaders who allowed bold questions to be asked inside conservative institutions, thank you.

To the technologists who believed that finance could think, not just process, thank you.

To the regulators who understand that innovation and responsibility must evolve together, thank you.

To the readers of my previous books, your engagement across geographies reminded me that the future of banking is a shared global journey.

And to my family for tolerating the late nights, the scattered notes, and the obsessive rewrites—your quiet belief made this manuscript possible.

Banking may be transforming through intelligence.

But transformation always begins with people.

This book is for those courageous enough to build what does not yet exist.

Author's Note

This book is not about software.

It is about a turning point.

For centuries, banks were defined by vaults, marble floors, and physical ledgers. Later, by data centres and mobile apps. But beneath every era, one constant remained:

Decisions determined destiny.

Who receives credit.

Who bears risk.

Where capital flows.

How value is measured.

For most of history, those decisions were human. Then, they became assisted by systems. Now, they are increasingly made or shaped by intelligence.

We are standing at the edge of a structural shift in financial history. Not a feature release, not a product upgrade, but a redesign of the core logic of banking itself.

Over more than two decades working across Africa, Asia, the Middle East and Europe, I have seen institutions attempt digital transformation. Some succeeded. Many modernised their interfaces while leaving their decision engines untouched.

But artificial intelligence does not simply digitise banking.

It rewires it.

An app does not define the AI-First Bank. It is defined by a living intelligence layer embedded across credit, compliance, liquidity, capital allocation, and customer experience.

This shift will not be optional.

But how we implement it—responsibly or recklessly—is entirely our choice.

This book is written for those who intend to choose wisely.

Preface

The first banks were built on trust and ledgers.

The next were built on code and connectivity.

The next will be built on intelligence.

Digital banking changed how customers interact with finance. It reduced friction, expanded inclusion, and placed services in the palm. But beneath the smooth glass screens, many institutions remained structurally unchanged.

Rules hard-coded decades ago.

Credit models designed for slower economies.

Quarterly risk assessments in real-time markets.

Digital on the surface. Industrial at the core.

Artificial intelligence changes the equation, not because it is faster, but because it learns.

For the first time, financial institutions can evolve continuously. Risk can be recalibrated dynamically. Liquidity can be anticipated instead of reacting to. Fraud can be detected before it materialises. Capital can be allocated with precision rather than approximation.

But intelligence without wisdom is dangerous.

Automation without accountability is destabilising.

The AI-First Bank must not simply be intelligent.

It must be ethical.

Transparent.

Governed.

This book is an exploration of that future—a future where banking becomes less about products and more about decisions; less about channels and more about cognition.

The institutions that understand this shift will not merely adapt.

They will define the financial architecture of the next generation.

Introduction

Banking is no longer about branches.

It is no longer about apps.

It is no longer even about banks.

It is about decisions.

Every financial system, no matter how complex, ultimately reduces to a sequence of judgements: who to trust, how much to lend, what to price, when to intervene, where to allocate capital. For centuries, these judgements were human, constrained by limited information and institutional memory.

Digital transformation gave us speed.

Artificial intelligence gives us foresight.

The centre of gravity in banking is shifting from product design to decision design, from workflow efficiency to intelligence architecture, from reporting what happened to predicting and shaping what will happen.

The AI-First Bank is not a theoretical construct. It is already emerging quietly in underwriting engines that learn, in liquidity models that predict stress, in compliance systems that monitor behaviour in real time.

But there is a profound question beneath the technology:

If algorithms increasingly influence financial outcomes, who governs the algorithms?

This book attempts to answer that question. It maps the shift from digital banking to AI-First banking. It outlines the architectural layers, governance frameworks, and leadership mindsets required. It challenges institutions to rethink not only their systems, but their philosophy.

Because once intelligence becomes the core infrastructure of finance, the stakes are no longer operational.

They are systemic.

CHAPTER 1

Digital Is Dead: Why AI Has Already Replaced the Digital Transformation Agenda

"Digital transformed the channel. AI transforms the institution."

This chapter argues that digital transformation has reached its natural limits: it modernised channels, interfaces, and workflows, but it never changed the underlying intelligence of the bank. As AI reshapes every function—from risk to credit to fraud—the agenda is no longer about digitising processes, but about rethinking how decisions are made, how value is created, and how financial institutions operate at the atomic level. The chapter sets the tone for the book: digital is efficiency; AI is reinvention.

For more than a decade, bank boardrooms celebrated digital transformation as the ultimate finish line—new apps launched, branches shrank, and customer journeys went online. Yet quietly, almost imperceptibly, a new wave began to rise beneath the surface: algorithms started making better predictions than seasoned teams, fraud models detected anomalies humans couldn't see, and customer expectations shifted from "online banking" to "instant, invisible, intelligent." By the time most institutions declared digital victory, a new race had already begun, and digital was no longer enough.

For more than a decade, "digital transformation" dominated the vocabulary of global banking. It appeared in every board briefing, every strategy offsite, every RFP document, every vendor pitch, and every conference keynote. Banks used it to justify multi-million-dollar budgets, major reorganisations, new CX initiatives, and sweeping technology refreshes. Digital transformation became the strategic north star for an entire generation of executives.

But repetition does not make something transformative.

In reality, digital transformation was far less revolutionary than banks believed. It fixed the visible weaknesses, slow channels, paper-heavy processes, and branch dependency, but did not address the intellectual weaknesses:

how banks think, decide, learn, and respond to risk. The digital era modernised the façade, not the foundation. It made banking faster, more convenient, and more accessible, but not smarter.

By the mid-2020s, a series of forces converged—technological, economic, regulatory, and behavioural—that rendered digital transformation insufficient. Banks realised that while they had modernised their channels, they had not modernised their judgement. While they digitised processes, they had not digitised intelligence. While they improved distribution, they had not improved decision-making. Customers could now access banking easily, but banks still struggled to understand customers meaningfully.

The world outgrew digital, and AI quietly replaced it.

Artificial intelligence did not simply add new functionality; it reshaped the definition of transformation itself. AI did not make apps faster; it made decisions faster. AI did not reduce clicks; it reduced uncertainty. AI did not automate tasks; it reinvented institutional cognition. AI did not improve compliance workflows; it changed the very nature of compliance.

Digital transformation solved **access**.

AI transformation solves **understanding** (see Figure 1.1).

It is essential to understand how AI has already become the new operating system of financial institutions, and why banks must now shift from digital-first thinking to intelligence-first architecture to remain competitive in the decade ahead.

Figure 1.1 – The Shift from Digital to A

Category	PAST (Pre-Digital)	DIGITAL ERA (Last 10–15 yrs)	AI ERA (Emerging / Now)
Core Features	• Branch networks • Physical forms • Manual processes • Paper statements	• Mobile apps • Internet banking • Omni-channel UX • Cloud + APIs	• Decision engines • AI-driven models • Real-time learning • Behavioural analytics
Competition On	• Presence • Coverage	• Experience • Convenience	• Intelligence • Accuracy and Adaptation

The Digital Era Was Defensive – A Race to Stay in the Game

Digital transformation was not born from imagination. It was born from fear. Fear of losing customers to fintechs, fear of becoming irrelevant in a mobile-first world, fear of being outpaced by nimble startups with no legacy baggage, fear of regulators mandating modernisation before banks could strategise it.

1. Fintechs Forced Banks Into Speed and Convenience

   In the early days, fintechs exploded across Africa, Asia, Europe and Latin America. From M-Pesa to Revolut, Nubank to Chime, Paytm to Flutterwave, these platforms demonstrated how banking could work if built from a blank canvas:

   - Instant onboarding
   - Zero paperwork
   - 24/7 availability
   - Clean interfaces

- Transparent fees
- Two-click payments
- In-app support

A young graduate in Lagos could open a digital wallet in 90 seconds. A freelancer in Warsaw could get a virtual card immediately. A small business in São Paulo could receive payments without a merchant contract. These experiences made traditional banks feel outdated, slow, bureaucratic and inconvenient.

Banks did not choose digital transformation proactively. They were dragged into it.

2. Bigtech Redefined Service Expectations

   Customers no longer compare banks with other banks. They compared banks with the experiences they had:

   - Amazon
   - Uber
   - Netflix
   - Spotify
   - Apple
   - Airbnb

   These companies introduced the idea that technology should anticipate your needs, not merely respond to them. If an Uber driver could be matched in three seconds, why did a bank still take three days to process a credit limit increase? If Netflix could recommend the perfect film, why couldn't a bank personalise products with similar precision?

   The gap between what customers expected and what banks delivered widened dramatically.

3. Regulators Pushed Banks Into Digitisation

   Long before banks felt ready, regulators had already rewritten the rules of the game.

- Digital KYC
- Cybersecurity requirements
- Real-time transaction monitoring
- Data protection mandates
- Cloud-computing policies

Suddenly, compliance departments found themselves fighting a battle they couldn't win with paper files and manual workflows. Every new circular, every new requirement, carried the same message: the old system cannot keep up.

What followed wasn't a strategic leap into the future; it was a race to avoid falling behind. Banks digitised not because they were visionary, but because regulation demanded a level of scale, precision, and speed that only technology could deliver.

Digitisation became the new survival code.

Digital Was a Response to a Threat, Not a Vision for the Future

Banks digitised, because the alternative was extinction. Digital transformation was defensive modernisation, not imaginative reinvention.

- Digital delivered
- Cleaner interfaces
- Faster transactions
- Improved channel coverage
- Reduced branch dependency
- Automated workflows
- Basic chatbots
- Cloud-based scalability

But the brain of the bank remained analogue.

Digital did **not** transform:

- How risk is understood
- How credit is priced
- How fraud patterns are identified
- How identity is validated over time
- How limit decisions adapt
- How compliance learns
- How treasury predicts liquidity
- How debt is collected with empathy
- How customer behaviour is interpreted

Digital made banking **faster**.

AI makes banking **smarter.**

A digital bank is simply a traditional bank delivered through a screen.

This is why digital reached an endpoint.

Why Digital Is Over: Three Irreversible Shifts

Around 2023–2025, global banking crossed an invisible threshold. Three structural changes made digital insufficient and repositioned AI as the only viable transformation agenda.

Shift 1: Interfaces No Longer Differentiate, Intelligence Does

The digital race turned banking into a design competition.

Banks hired UX designers, sprint coaches, design-thinking consultants and app modernisation firms. They rebuilt journeys to reduce clicks, minimised input fields, added OCR scanning, introduced dark mode and built faster login flows.

But by 2025, every bank's app looked and behaved the same.

- Onboard in minutes
- Instant transfers
- In-app statements
- Digital KYC
- Clean dashboards
- Budget tools
- Notifications

The interface war is over.

The new battlefield is invisible, buried deep inside the decision-making logic.

Customers no longer choose banks based on appearance; they choose banks based on the quality and speed of decisions.

- How quickly can I get approved?
- How precisely can fraud be prevented?
- How personalised is my pricing?
- How dynamic are my limits?
- How seamless is my global identity?
- How proactively am I protected from risk?

Design is cosmetic.

Intelligence is competitive. (see Figure 1.2)

Figure 1.2 – Digital vs AI in the Bank's Architecture

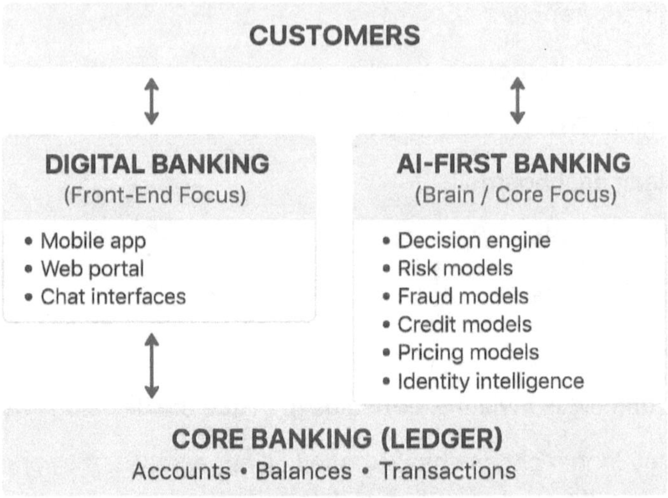

Shift 2: The Customer Became Global – Digital Banking Stayed Domestic

The average customer today is globally entangled in ways no bank anticipated:

- Lives in Nairobi.
- Works for a UK company.
- Gets paid in EUR.
- Freelances for a US client.
- Pays rent in KES.
- Travels through Dubai.
- Invests in India.
- Shops from China.
- Saves in USD.

Similarly, modern businesses run cross-border operations organically;

- Multi-country vendors
- Multi-currency invoices

- Remote-first staff
- Global logistics
- Regional tax exposure

But banking systems remained stubbornly local.

Digital banking was built for a world where a customer lived, earned, spent and invested in the same jurisdiction.

That world is gone.

AI banking, however, can:

- Evaluate risk globally.
- Detect fraud across networks.
- Validate identity across borders.
- Assign limits based on global patterns.
- Understand behaviour, irrespective of nationality.

Figure 1.3 – The Customer Is Global, Digital Banking Is Local

CUSTOMER REALITY (GLOBAL)	**DIGITAL BANK** (LOCAL)	**AI-FIRST BANK** (GLOBAL BEHAVIOUR)
• Lives in Nairobi	• National KYC	• Cross-border identity graph
• Earns in GBP	• Domestic fraud rules	• Behavioural risk modelling
• Paid in EUR	• Local scoring models	• Global anomaly detection
• Invests in INR	• Local limits only	• Real-time, adaptive limits
• Spends in USD	• Local compliance	• Continuous, multi-country KYC
• Works remotely for US firm	• Geographic identity	

Shift 3: Digital Products Were Static, AI Products Are Adaptive

Even the best digital products of the 2010s and 2020s shared one characteristic: static logic.

- Fixed credit limits
- Fixed interest rates
- Fixed risk thresholds
- Fixed onboarding steps
- Fixed fraud rules
- Static KYC
- Static pricing

Banks could change these rules, but only through manual updates, committees, version releases or annual reviews.

- Static logic cannot thrive in a dynamic world.
- AI transforms every banking product into a living, evolving organism:
- Credit limits adjust daily, not annually.
- Models retrain hourly, not quarterly.
- Pricing adapts individually, not in slabs.
- Fraud rules evolve with patterns, not with policy memos.
- Segmentation becomes fluid, not category-based.

Figure 1.4 – Static Products vs Adaptive Products

DIGITAL PRODUCT (STATIC)	AI PRODUCT (ADAPTIVE)
• Fixed credit limit	• Limit evolves daily
• Fixed pricing	• Behaviour-driven rates
• Static segmentation	• Dynamic micro-segments
• Periodic KYC	• Always-on KYC
• Rule-based fraud	• Anomaly-based fraud

STATIC:

——————————→ | Minor updates

ADAPTIVE:

Launch → Learn → Adjust → Learn → Predict

The Core Difference: Rules vs Learning Systems

Digital transformation was rooted in rules. Banks built giant rule factories, thousands of IF-THEN logic blocks operationalised through decades of committees and risk memos.

Rules Are Finite. Models Are Infinite

A rule engine can only respond to scenarios that humans have predicted.

A model can respond to scenarios humans have never imagined.

Rules break under novelty.

Models thrive under novelty.

Rules assume.

Models infer.

Rules require manual updates.

Models self-improve.

Why Rules Failed Digital Banking

- rigid
- brittle
- biased
- Unable to detect anomalous behaviour
- easily bypassed
- Impossible to scale
- Slow to evolve

Why AI Models Succeed

- Contextual
- adaptive
- continuously learning
- personalised
- Probabilistic
- Behaviourally aware
- pattern-sensitive

A rule might say, "If the transaction exceeds X, trigger an alert."

A model might detect that:

  - The user has shifted spending patterns
  - is in a new geography
  - is interacting with a new merchant type
  - at a suspicious time
  - on a device with a new network fingerprint

Rules think in isolation.

Models think in connection.

Figure 1.5 – Rules vs Models in Decisioning

RULE ENGINE (OLD)	MODEL ENGINE (NEW)
Input → Iff–Then Rules Decision	Input → ML Model → Prediction
• Manual logic • Finite conditions • Fragile under new behaviour • High false positives/ negatives	• Learns from data • Detects anomalies • Adapts across contexts • Predictive accuracy

Input → ML Model → Prediction

AI Has Already Moved from the Edge to the Core

For most digital transformations, AI was treated like a cosmetic enhancement.

Banks used AI for:

- Chatbots
- Email classification
- Marketing recommendations
- Simple scoring

But these were side features, cosmetic layers added to a conventional architecture.

By 2025, something changed.

AI migrated from the edge to the core.

AI now drives:

- credit
- fraud
- AML
- onboarding
- identity
- pricing
- collections
- treasury

AI is not another layer.

AI is the new architecture.

Figure 1.6 – AI at the Edge vs AI in the Core

PAST: AI ON THE EDGE	NOW: AI IN THE CORE
Channels → Chatbots → Ledger	Decision → AI Decision Engine Decision Engine Includes: • Credit ML • Fraud ML • AML ML • Pricing ML • Identity Signals • Risk Predictions

Decisioning is the New Core Banking

Traditional core banking was built around:

- Accounts

- Balances
- Transactions.
- Products

But banking is not about accounts; it is about decisions.

- Should we onboard this customer?
- Should we approve this transaction?
- What limit should we assign?
- What price should we offer?
- Is this customer risky?
- Is this behaviour anomalous?
- Should we escalate this transaction?

These are decision questions, not ledger questions.

AI-first architecture treats the decision engine as the heart of the bank.

Figure 1.7 – Old Core vs New Core

OLD CORE	NEW CORE
Customers	Customers
↓	↓
Accounts	Behaviour
↓	↓
Transactions	Predictions
↓	↓
Ledger	Decision Engine
	↓
	Ledger

Why Banks Still Feel Behind, Even After Digital Transformation

A paradox emerged in the 2020s.

Banks invested billions into digital transformation. They built modern apps, automated workflows, cloud-native platforms, API gateways, and sleek user journeys.

And yet...

Internally, banks felt:

- slow
- reactive
- risk-heavy
- operationally rigid
- dependent on manual decisions.
- unable to adapt in real-time

Why?

Because digital fixed **execution**, not **judgement**.

Digital has improved the way banks deliver.

AI improves the way banks decide.

Digital transformation made banks efficient.

AI makes banks intelligent.

Most banks remain digitally mature, but intelligence-poor.

AI Is Rewriting Banking at a Molecular Level

AI is not a technology upgrade; it is a cognitive upgrade.

Risk

From static scorecards → to dynamic probability models.

Fraud

From reactive alerts → to pre-emptive anomaly detection.

Compliance

From retrospective checks → to continuous monitoring.

Identity

From document-based → to behavioural signatures.

Credit

From snapshot underwriting → to real-time scoring.

Pricing

From fixed slabs → to personalised curves.

Products

From predefined → to self-adjusting.

Treasury

From historical patterns → to global forecasting.

AI does not automate the bank.

AI re-architects the bank.

The End of Digital: A Definitive Conclusion

Digital transformation solved the problems of the past.

AI solves the problems of the future.

Digital:

- Fixed access
- Improved speed
- Enabled scale
- Made banking smoother

But digital cannot:

- Understand behaviour
- Predict risk.
- Globalise identity

- Personalise pricing
- Detect fraud in advance
- Learn continuously
- Adapt instantly

Digital was the warm-up.

AI is the main event.

Figure 1.8 – Digital Was the Warm-Up, AI Is the Main Event

PRE–2015	DIGITAL ADOPTION
2015–2025	DIGITAL TRANSFORMATION
2025–2030	AI

DIGITAL = Experience revolution
AI = Intelligence revolution

The New Transformation Agenda: Intelligence-First Banking

The next decade of banking will be shaped by institutions that build around intelligence, not channels.

The shift is from:

- Channels → to decisions
- Workflows → to predictions
- Documents → to behaviour

- Rules → to models
- Products → to systems
- Infrastructure → to intelligence

The question is no longer:

"What is our digital roadmap?"

The question is now:

"What is our intelligence roadmap?"

Digital banking closed one chapter.

AI banking begins next.

What Comes Next

In Chapter Two, we will explore:

The operating model of an AI-first institution

- New organisational structures
- The intelligence layer stack
- Model governance frameworks
- Behavioural identity systems
- Adaptive credit architecture
- Real-time risk and fraud engines
- Data orchestration for continuous learning

The shift from digital-first to AI-first is not a minor upgrade.

It is a reinvention of the bank from the inside out.

The future does not belong to digital banks.

The future belongs to intelligent banks.

"Digital made banks faster. AI makes them wiser. And in this era, wisdom is the ultimate competitive advantage."

CHAPTER 2

Anatomy of the AI-First Bank

"Banks were built on processes. AI-first banks are built on decisions."

This chapter introduces the blueprint of the AI-first bank, a model built not on processes or departments, but on real-time, intelligence-driven decision-making. It breaks down the organisational, architectural, and cultural layers of an institution where intelligence flows horizontally across every interaction and vertically through every system. It contrasts legacy operating models with AI-native ones, showing how banks evolve from slow, linear structures to adaptive, learning organisations.

Walk inside an AI-first bank, and you won't find the familiar maze of departments, committees and handoffs. Instead, you'll see something almost biological—systems learning in real time, decisions flowing like electrical signals, and intelligence embedded into every interaction. The institution behaves less like a bank and more like a living organism. The old banking blueprint collapses, replaced by an architecture where intelligence, not hierarchy, drives the operating model.

In Chapter One, we established a simple truth: **digital transformation is complete**, and the era of interface-driven innovation is over. AI has emerged not as an extension of digital but as the new foundation of financial institutions.

This chapter answers the next obvious question:

What Does an AI-first Bank Look Like?

What does it mean—architecturally, operationally, culturally—to run a bank where intelligence is not a feature but the core? What does the institution look like when decision-making—not channels, not products, not UX—becomes the central organ of the enterprise? How does governance change? How does risk transform? How do teams evolve? How does technology realign?

For the first time in 50 years, banks have the opportunity to redesign themselves from the inside out—not around ledgers or accounts, but around **behaviour, predictions, models**, and **intelligence flows**.

The AI-first bank is not a digital bank with better algorithms.

It is a fundamentally different organism—faster, lighter, more adaptive, and more contextually aware.

This chapter provides a blueprint.

1. The AI-First Bank Is Built Around a "Decision Engine" (Not a Core System)

For decades, the heart of the bank was the **core banking system**—the ledger. The institution revolved around accounts, balances, products, and transactions. Everything else was layered on top of it.

In an AI-first bank, the ledger is no longer the centre.

The **decision engine** becomes the centre.

The decision engine governs:

- onboarding
- identity
- fraud
- risk
- credit
- limits
- pricing
- collections
- product personalisation
- AML
- treasury forecasts

Where traditional banks organised their architecture around data storage, AI-first banks organise their architecture around data interpretation.

The decision engine becomes the institutional brain.

Figure 2.1 – From Ledger-Centric to Decision-Centric Architecture

LEDGER-FIRST ARCHITECTURE (OLD)

[Channels] --> [Middleware] --> [Ledger] --> [Decisions]

- Ledger is central.
- Decisions are downstream.
- Human-heavy judgement.

DECISION-FIRST ARCHITECTURE (AI-FIRST)

[Channels] --> [Decision Engine] --> [Ledger]

Decision Engine Includes:

- Identity models
- Fraud models
- Risk models
- Credit models
- Pricing models
- Collections models
- AML/compliance models

2. The Four Pillars of an AI-First Bank

Every AI-first institution is built on four foundational pillars:

1. Behavioural Identity
2. Continuous Risk and Fraud Intelligence
3. Dynamic Credit and Pricing Engines
4. Adaptive Product Systems

Let's explore each in detail.

2.1 Pillar One: Behavioural Identity (The New KYC)

Traditional identity is static:

- passport
- ID number
- utility bill
- address
- employer
- national ID database

These signals are weak. They can only confirm who you were at a point in time, not who you are today.

AI-first identity is dynamic.

It includes:

- Device intelligence
- Geolocation patterns
- Typing cadence
- Behavioural consistency
- Network graph associations
- Transaction patterns
- Spending rhythms
- Employer stability
- Payment velocity
- Revenue volatility
- Sentiment signals

Identity becomes a behavioural signature, constantly updating, continuously validated.

Why Behavioural Identity Matters:

- Prevents sophisticated fraud.
- Enables cross-border onboarding.
- Powers global compliance.
- Reduces document friction.
- Allows real-time limit adjustments.
- Improves creditworthiness assessment.

Banks that cling to document-based identity will always lag behind attackers and global customers.

Behavioural identity is the foundation of the AI-first institution.

Figure 2.2 – Document Identity vs Behavioural Identity

DOCUMENT IDENTITY (OLD)

- Passport / ID
- Utility bill
- Selfie + OCR
- Static checks
- Easily forged
- One-time verification

BEHAVIOURAL IDENTITY (AI-FIRST)

- Device signals
- Location patterns
- Typing cadence
- Spending graph
- Social graph
- Risk velocity
- Real-time monitoring
- Continuous KYC

2.2 Pillar Two: Continuous Risk and Fraud Intelligence

Traditional risk and fraud systems are episodic.

They rely on:

- Threshold rules
- Periodic reviews
- Limited variables
- Static segments
- Retrospective analyses

Risk in traditional banks is fundamentally backwards-looking.

AI-first risk is forward-looking.

It uses:

- Anomaly detection
- Graph-based fraud intelligence
- cash flow prediction
- Cluster-based segmentation
- Dynamic risk scoring
- Network intelligence

Fraud Becomes A Network Problem, Not A Customer Problem

Fraudsters do not operate alone. Criminal networks have patterns, shared devices, shared IP footprints, and shared behavioural attributes. Rules cannot detect these patterns. Models can.

Risk Becomes A Behavioural Forecast, Not A Static Rating

The bank understands:

- How likely repayment is tomorrow.
- How volatility is evolving.

- When a customer is entering financial stress.
- When behaviour deviates from historic rhythms.

Risk becomes predictive, not reactive.

Figure 2.3 – Periodic Risk vs Continuous Risk

PERIODIC RISK (OLD)

- Annual scoring
- Static models
- Fixed thresholds
- Manual investigations
- Local-only signals

CONTINUOUS RISK (AI-FIRST)

- Daily risk score updates
- Real-time data feeds
- Behaviour-drift detection
- Graph intelligence
- Cross-border signals

2.3 Pillar Three: Dynamic Credit and Personalised Pricing

Traditional credit is rigid:

- Scorecards
- Fixed policies
- Fixed interest rates
- Long underwriting cycles
- Limited variables

AI-first credit is fluid:

- Cash flow-based underwriting
- Income prediction

- Dynamic risk estimation
- Behavioural repayment models
- Micro-limit adjustments
- Pricing elasticity models

AI-First Pricing is Individualised

Every customer gets a pricing curve, not a pricing slab.

AI-first Limits Evolve Daily

A customer's limit is not a number; it is a living output of behaviour.

AI-first Credit is Global

A Kenyan living in Dubai, earning in GBP, and transacting in USD should not need three different credit profiles. AI merges these signals seamlessly.

This is one of the biggest value unlocks of the next decade.

Figure 2.4 – Static Credit vs Dynamic Credit

STATIC CREDIT (OLD)

- Score <600 = reject
- Annual credit review
- Fixed limit for 12 months
- Scorecard-based tiers

DYNAMIC CREDIT (AI-FIRST)

- Real-time affordability
- Weekly limit adjustments
- Cash flow prediction
- Behavioural risk score
- Personalised pricing curve

2.4 Pillar Four: Adaptive Product Systems

Digital banking products are static:

- one type of savings account
- one loan template
- Fixed fees
- Fixed pricing
- Predefined terms

AI-first products evolve like software.

They adapt based on:

- Transaction patterns
- Financial resilience
- Customer goals
- Income changes
- Spending rhythms
- Risk evolution

In the AI-first world:

- Products update themselves.
- Journeys self-optimise.
- Offers personalised dynamic content.
- Terms evolve with behaviour.

A product is no longer a product.

It is a **system**, a network of adaptive parameters optimised by models.

3. The AI-First Operating Model: How the Institution Runs

Transforming architecture is only half the battle.

The real transformation happens in **how the institution operates.**

An AI-first bank requires:

1. New teams
2. New processes
3. New governance
4. New rhythms of execution

Let's examine each.

3.1 New Teams: The Intelligence Organisation

Traditional banks have:

- IT
- Risk
- Credit
- Fraud
- Compliance
- Operations

AI-first banks add the Intelligence Organisation:

1. **Model Development Teams**

   Build and train models (fraud, risk, credit, pricing, identity).

2. **Model Monitoring Teams**

   Track drift, anomalies, false positives, errors, bias.

3. **Data Engineering Teams**

   Build pipelines, ingestion, real-time data streams.

4. **Intelligence Product Managers**

   Define model goals, outcomes, and use cases.

5. **Model Governance and Audit Units**

   Ensure transparency, fairness, and explainability.

6. **Behavioural Scientists**

   Interpret customer signals and cluster patterns.

7. **Decision Strategy Teams**

   Tune model outputs into real-world decisions.

This is a new organisational layer, one that did not exist in the digital era.

3.2 New Processes: Continuous Intelligence Delivery (CID)

Digital transformation used Agile and Scrum.

AI-first transformation uses **CID**.

CID = Continuous Intelligence Delivery

It includes:

- Continuous experimentation
- Continuous model testing
- Continuous deployment
- Continuous retraining
- Continuous governance
- Continuous drift detection

Every week:

- Models update
- Limits adjust
- Risk evolves
- Fraud patterns shift
- Customer behaviour changes

The AI-first bank operates like a real-time organism.

Figure 2.5 – Agile vs Continuous Intelligence Delivery (CID)

AGILE (DIGITAL ERA)

Plan → Build → Test → Deploy → Review

(2–6 week cycles)

CID (AI-FIRST ERA)

Monitor → Predict → Adapt → Retrain → Reinforce

(Continuous loop – daily or hourly)

3.3 New Governance: Model Governance Councils

In digital banking, governance controls processes.

In AI banking, governance controls **intelligence**.

Model Governance Councils oversee

- Model fairness
- Model explainability
- Drift thresholds
- Decision accuracy
- Regulatory compliance
- Transparency requirements
- Override policies

Model Governance Also Sets

- Monitoring SLAs
- Bias alerts
- Retraining schedules
- Cross-jurisdictional risk controls

The regulator of the future will not ask,

"How do you process KYC?"

but rather

"How do your models make decisions?"

Governance is shifting from process oversight to intelligence oversight.

3.4 New Rhythms: Decisions Become Living Entities

In traditional banks:

- Policies change annually.
- Fraud rules adjust quarterly.
- Credit models update annually.
- Risk thresholds review biannually.

In AI-first banks:

- Limits adjust hourly.
- Fraud models retrain automatically.
- Pricing adapts per transaction.
- Onboarding pathways shift in real time.
- KYC becomes perpetual.

The institution becomes fluid, dynamic and continuously learning.

4. The AI-First Technology Stack: The Intelligence Layer

AI-first banking requires a completely new stack—one built on intelligence, not infrastructure.

The Intelligence Stack has seven layers:

1. Data Ingestion Layer
2. Real-Time Stream Processing
3. Feature Engineering Layer

4. Model Training and Retraining Layer
5. Model Serving Layer
6. Decision Orchestration Layer
7. Feedback and Learning Layer

Let's break this down.

4.1 Layer One: Data Ingestion

The AI-first bank collects:

- Transactional data
- Device data
- Behavioural data
- Biometric signals
- Employer data
- Income flows
- Credit bureau reports
- Network intelligence
- Geographic risk data
- Merchant risk patterns
- Cross-border signals

Banks that do not ingest enough data cannot build accurate intelligence.

4.2 Layer Two: Real-Time Stream Processing

AI-first banks cannot rely on batch data.

They use stream engines to process:

- Velocity

- Frequency
- Drift
- Anomalies
- Behavioural events
- Risk signals
- Fraud alerts

This enables instant decisions.

4.3 Layer Three: Feature Engineering

Features are the building blocks of intelligence.

Traditional banks use 5–15 variables.

AI-first banks use 200–2,000+ behavioural features.

Examples:

- Spending entropy
- Income volatility
- Repayment cadence
- Geographic consistency
- Session friction
- Merchant diversity
- Device trust score

These features drive model performance.

4.4 Layer Four: Model Training and Retraining

Models must be retrained on:

- New fraud patterns

- New risk conditions
- New customer behaviour
- Economic shifts
- Seasonal changes

Retraining cycles move from:

annual → to monthly → to weekly → to automated continuous retraining

4.5 Layer Five: Model Serving Layer

This layer ensures models respond in milliseconds.

Banks cannot run models that take seconds.

Instant decisions require:

- GPU optimisation
- low-latency model servers
- caching strategies
- pre-computed features

4.6 Layer Six: Decision Orchestration

This is where the magic happens.

Orchestration ensures:

- Model outputs become decisions
- Decisions follow policies
- Exceptions escalate
- Human overrides log automatically
- Risk tolerances adjust

Figure 2.6 – Decision Orchestration Layer

Inputs:

- Risk Score
- Fraud Score
- Identity Score
- Credit Prediction

Decision Orchestration:

- Combine signals
- Apply policy rules
- Trigger workflows
- Escalate exceptions

Outputs:

- Approve
- Decline
- Review
- Adjust Limit
- Apply Pricing

4.7 Layer Seven: Feedback and Learning

AI-first banks continuously collect:

- False positives
- False negatives
- Override reasons
- Customer behaviour, post-decision

This creates a **learning loop**.

Models improve every day from outcomes.

5. The AI-First Bank: A Real-World Example Scenario

Let's walk through a real-world scenario to illustrate the difference between digital and AI-first architectures.

Scenario: A New Customer Applies for a Credit Card

Digital Bank (Old Approach)

1. Customer submits ID
2. System fetches credit bureau score
3. Scorecard checks:
   - If credit score > threshold → approve
   - Else → reject or manual review
4. Fraud check uses rules:
   - If device = new AND amount > threshold → alert
5. Limit assigned from fixed slabs
6. Pricing set from predefined tiers

Outcome:

- Approval takes hours or days
- Limited accuracy
- High false positives
- Static limit and pricing

AI-First Bank (New Approach)

1. Customer begins onboarding
2. Behavioural identity engine activates:
   - Device trustworthiness
   - GPS pattern

   - Typing cadence
   - Interaction rhythm
3. Real-time fraud engine evaluates:
   - Velocity anomalies
   - Network graph patterns
   - Shared risk clusters
4. Credit model predicts:
   - Income stability
   - Affordability
   - Risk over the next 90 days
   - Repayment likelihood
5. Pricing engine computes:
   - Personalised interest rate
   - Fee structure
   - Credit line trajectory
6. Decision engine produces:
   - Instant approval
   - Dynamic limit
   - Personalised pricing
   - Fraud-safe onboarding
   - Global identity consistency

Outcome:

- Decision in 1–3 seconds
- Higher approval rates with lower risk
- Lower fraud losses

- Better customer experience
- Dynamic adjustments over time

The AI-first bank does not just make faster decisions; it makes **superior** decisions.

6. The AI-First Compliance Institution

AI-first compliance is a complete paradigm shift.

Traditional compliance:

- rule-based
- periodic
- reactive
- investigative

AI-first compliance:

- continuous
- predictive
- behavioural
- , pattern-based

Instead of investigating suspicious transactions after they occur, AI-first banks detect suspicious behavioural patterns before the transactions happen.

Compliance Shifts From

- documentation → to behaviour
- rules → to models
- sampling → to continuous monitoring
- static checks → to anomaly detection
- manual review → to automated interpretation

Regulators across the world, from MAS to FCA to CBK, are already shifting towards AI supervision, expecting banks to adopt explainable AI and continuous, risk-based monitoring.

7. The Culture of an AI-First Bank

Technology alone cannot create an AI-first bank.

Culture makes or breaks the transformation.

An AI-first culture has six attributes:

1. **Data Humility**

   Decisions follow data – not hierarchy.

2. **Experimentation**

   Hypothesis → Test → Learn → Iterate

3. **Model Literacy**

   Executives understand risk scoring, drift, and AI ethics.

4. **Interdisciplinary Teams**

   Risk + Data + Engineering + Product + Compliance work as one

5. **Real-Time Reflexes**

   Daily decision improvements, not annual policy changes

6. **Ethics and Transparency**

   AI must be explainable, fair, and governed.

Banks that do not transform culturally will fail technologically.

8. The AI-First Bank as a Living System

The AI-first bank is not a static organisation.

It is a living, breathing, adaptive organism.

It learns.

It adjusts.

It predicts.

It evolves.

It reacts.

It self-corrects.

It self-optimises.

It becomes more intelligent with every interaction.

Banks have spent a century acting like bureaucratic machines.

The future demands that they behave like intelligent organisms.

Conclusion: The Anatomy of the AI-First Institution

To summarise:

- The ledger is no longer the core; the decision engine is.
- Identity is no longer document-based; it's behavioural.
- Risk is no longer periodic; it's continuous.
- Credit is no longer static; it's dynamic.
- Pricing is no longer generic; it's personalised.
- Products are no longer fixed; they are adaptive.
- Compliance is no longer reactive; it's predictive.
- Technology is no longer infrastructure-driven; it's intelligence-driven.
- Culture is no longer hierarchical; it's experimental.

Chapter Two gave you the architecture, operating model and intelligence stack of the AI-first bank.

Chapter Three will explore **the AI-first product universe**—a blueprint for remittances, lending, SME banking, treasury, identity systems, and cross-border finance in the intelligence era.

"A bank built on data survives. A bank built on intelligence leads."

CHAPTER 3

Decision Intelligence: The New Core Banking

"The bank with the smartest decisions, not the fastest app, wins the decade."

In this chapter, the centre of gravity in banking shifts from product systems to decision systems. It explains why decision intelligence becomes the new "core banking," powering underwriting, pricing, onboarding, fraud, risk, and customer experience. The chapter highlights how banks can build a unified intelligence layer that sits above channels and systems, enabling smarter, faster, more contextual actions that traditional workflow engines cannot match.

Before the first loan is issued, the first payment is cleared, or the first customer is onboarded, one thing happens: a decision. Yet banks have spent decades perfecting products and channels while leaving decision-making buried in spreadsheets, rules, and legacy workflows. In an intelligence-driven world, the competitive battlefield shifts to a single question: who makes the smartest decisions at scale? The new core of the bank is not a system; it is a decision engine.

"In the digital era, banks digitised old products.

In the AI era, banks design products that behave like intelligent systems."

Digital transformation improved access.

AI transformation improves **adaptation, intelligence, precision and prediction**.

In this chapter, we explore how AI redefines the actual products banks deliver to customers.

Until now, banking products have been:

- fixed
- predefined
- static
- rule-based

Products did not evolve unless a human intervened.

They did not respond to the behaviour.

They did not improve themselves.

They did not learn.

AI-native products behave differently.

They are:

- dynamic
- adaptive
- self-optimising
- predictive
- personalised
- continuously improving

This chapter delves into five product domains that AI is transforming completely:

1. **Identity and Onboarding**
2. **Payments and Cross-Border Finance**
3. **Lending and Credit Systems**
4. **Fraud, Risk and Compliance Systems**
5. **Treasury, Liquidity and Financial Forecasting**

These pillars form the backbone of the AI-native banking product universe.

1. Identity and Onboarding: From KYC to Continuous Identity Intelligence

Identity is the foundation of every financial product.

But banks traditionally treat identity as a **moment**, not a **signal**.

KYC happens once.

Documentation is static.

Validation is manual.

Risk is snapshot-based.

This works only in a world where:

- Customers never change.
- Fraudsters are naive.
- Borders don't matter.
- Identity is fixed over time.

None of these is true anymore.

1.1 AI-Native Identity Is Continuous

AI-native identity systems treat identity as a continuous behavioural signal, a living profile that evolves with the customer's actions.

Identity signals include:

- Device fingerprinting
- Typing cadence
- Spending entropy
- Behavioural consistency
- Location patterns
- Network associations
- Social graph risk
- Transaction velocity
- Income traceability
- Merchant graph behaviour

Identity is not a document.

Identity is a **behavioural pattern**.

Figure 3.1 – Static Identity vs Continuous Identity

STATIC IDENTITY (DIGITAL)

- Passport
- ID number
- Utility bill
- OCR selfie check
- One-time KYC
- Manual periodic review

CONTINUOUS IDENTITY (AI-NATIVE)

- Device behaviour
- Typing cadence
- GPS consistency
- Social graph signals
- Income flow patterns
- Real-time KYC/KYB
- Continuous risk scoring

1.2 AI Enables Frictionless Global Onboarding

Traditional onboarding is adversarial:

- too many forms
- too much friction
- outdated questions

AI-native onboarding:

- auto-fills
- predicts missing fields
- adapts to friction points

- reduces drop-offs
- verifies identity through behavioural intelligence
- scores risk before asking for documents
- tailors onboarding flow to customer type

An SME in Lagos can onboard for a Dubai-based fintech using:

- director network signals
- historical payment flows
- device trust
- beneficiary patterns

AI removes geography from KYC.

1.3 Identity as a Multi-Layered Signal Graph

AI transforms identity into a **multi-layered intelligence graph**:

1. Who the customer is (baseline identity)
2. How the customer behaves (behaviour layer)
3. Who the customer interacts with (network layer)
4. How the customer evolves (drift layer)

This produces a holistic, continuously updating identity profile.

Figure 3.2 – The Identity Intelligence Graph

```
+-----------------------+
|   Baseline Identity   |
|  (Documents & Data)   |
+-----------+-----------+
            ↓
+-----------------------+
|   Behaviour Layer     |
| (Patterns & Signals)  |
+-----------+-----------+
            ↓
+-----------------------+
|    Network Layer      |
| (Connections & Links) |
+-----------+-----------+
            ↓
+-----------------------+
|    Drift Layer        |
| (Changes Over Time)   |
+-----------------------+
```

2. Infrastructure

Cross-border payments used to be:

- slow
- expensive
- opaque
- bureaucratic
- AI-native payment systems remove friction at every layer.

2.1 AI Builds a Global Customer Graph

Traditional banks evaluate payments at the transaction level.

AI-native banks evaluate payments at the **network level**:

- Who is paying whom
- At what rhythm
- With what purpose
- From what device
- Across what networks
- With what historical behaviour

This drastically reduces fraud, false positives and regulatory risk.

2.2 AI Improves FX and Routing Decisions

Digital banks follow fixed routing rules.

AI-native banks optimise routing in real time:

- Best corridor
- Lowest cost
- Highest compliance score
- Lowest risk
- Fastest clearing time
- Optimal liquidity path

AI can reduce cross-border costs by 40–60%.

2.3 AI Detects Illicit Networks Across Borders

Illicit networks use:

- Multiple devices

- Shared beneficiary accounts
- Layered merchants
- Small, repeated transactions

AI-native systems detect these patterns long before humans can.

Figure 3.3 – AI-Supported Cross-Border Network Detection

Transaction A ---> Device X ---> Beneficiary M

Transaction B ---> Device X ---> Beneficiary N

Transaction C ---> Device Y ---> Beneficiary M

AI finds:

- Shared device
- Shared beneficiary
- Velocity anomalies
- Risk clusters

2.4 Adaptive Limits for Cross-Border Transfers

Rather than fixed transfer caps:

- Limits adapt
- Based on risk
- Based on behaviour
- Based on volatility
- Based on compliance history

Every user gets a **personal risk-adjusted corridor**.

3. Lending and Credit Systems: Adaptive Underwriting and Behavioural Credit

Lending is the biggest product category AI is transforming.

Traditional credit:

- relies on static bureaus
- fixed scorecards
- annual reviews
- manual checks
- limited data

AI-native credit:

- dynamic
- continuous
- behaviour-based
- cash flow-driven
- predictive

3.1 AI Turns Cashflow Into a Predictive Asset

Instead of a credit score only, AI evaluates:

- income stability
- customer resilience
- repayment behaviour
- spending rhythms
- seasonality
- risk exposure
- external obligations
- real earnings vs declared earnings

AI reconstructs a **true financial portrait**.

Figure 3.4 – Behavioural Credit Model

Behavioural Inputs:

- spending patterns
- income volatility
- savings signals
- social graph stability
- merchant patterns
- repayment cadence
- device trust score

Model Outputs:

- probability of default
- recommended limit
- personalised pricing
- repayment prediction

3.2 Dynamic Limits: The Credit Line That Evolves

Static credit lines cause:

- unnecessary rejections
- higher risk exposure
- customer frustration

AI-native limits:

- increase when behaviour improves.
- decrease when risk rises.
- adjust weekly or daily.
- adapt to macroeconomic shifts.

The credit line becomes a **real-time contract** between the customer and the bank.

3.3 Personalised Pricing: AI's Most Important Advantage

Pricing used to be based on slabs:

- Prime +3%
- Prime +5%
- Prime +7%

AI-native pricing:

- dynamic
- adaptive
- personalised.
- behaviour-driven

Each customer gets a **unique pricing curve**:

- more stable = cheaper
- more volatile = slightly higher
- more predictable = lower risk premium
- lower fraud likelihood = tighter spread

AI increases fairness **and** profitability.

3.4 SME Credit Transformed

AI-native SME credit uses:

- invoice patterns
- cash flow cycles
- supplier graph
- customer concentration risk
- industry volatility
- seasonality

SMEs finally receive fair and fast credit decisions.

4. Fraud, Risk and Compliance: AI as Defensive and Offensive Intelligence

No part of banking benefits more from AI than fraud and compliance.

Traditional systems:

- reactive
- manual
- rules-driven
- full of false positives

AI-native systems:

- predictive
- intelligence-driven
- network-aware
- continuously learning

4.1 Fraud Detection as a Network Graph

Fraud is not about transactions—it's about connections.

AI identifies:

- shared devices
- shared IPs
- common merchants
- co-related geolocations
- temporal spikes
- behavioural drift

Figure 3.5 – Fraud Network Graph

Device A --> User 1 --> Merchant X
Device A --> User 2 --> Merchant Y
Device B --> User 3 --> Merchant X
AI detects:

- shared devices
- shared merchants
- transaction entropy
- velocity risk

4.2 AI Reduces False Positives

Rules usually fail because they are:

- too broad
- too narrow
- outdated
- blind to nuance

AI reduces false positives by up to 80% by:

- learning normal behaviour
- detecting anomalies
- combining multiple signals
- prioritising risk correctly

4.3 AI-Driven Compliance: Continuous AML

Traditional AML is slow:

- suspicious transaction reports
- manual investigation
- retrospective analysis

AI-native AML:

- continuous monitoring
- anomaly detection
- entity linking
- risk propagation
- real-time intervention

Compliance becomes a **real-time intelligence system**.

5. Treasury, Liquidity, and Financial Forecasting

Treasury has traditionally been:

- macro-driven
- spreadsheet-heavy
- dependent on analyst judgement

AI transforms treasury into a **predictive engine**.

5.1 Liquidity Forecasting

AI models:

- predict cash inflows
- forecast outflows
- detect liquidity stress
- simulate scenarios
- optimise reserves

Banks can optimise liquidity buffers more precisely.

5.2 FX and Hedging

AI evaluates:

- market signals
- sentiment
- volatility
- geopolitical risk
- customer transaction patterns

FX strategies become adaptive, not manual.

5.3 Asset-Liability Management (ALM)

AI improves ALM by:

- predicting rate sensitivity
- modelling behavioural deposits
- Forecasting prepayments
- stress-testing portfolios

ALM becomes real-time.

6. The AI-Native Product Design Process

AI-native product design fundamentally differs from digital product design.

Digital product design:

- journeys
- screens
- forms
- flows
- features

AI-native product design:

- signals
- models

- behaviours
- outcomes
- Feedback loops

Figure 3.6 – Digital Product vs AI-Native Product

DIGITAL PRODUCT

- Journey design
- Interface
- User flows
- Form fields
- Static logic
- Features

AI-NATIVE PRODUCT

- Behaviour models
- Prediction outputs
- Signals/features
- Decision rules
- Feedback loops
- Adaptive outcomes

7. How AI Rewrites Every Banking Product

We now examine how core banking products have changed completely.

7.1 Savings Accounts Become Intelligent Money Managers

A savings account can:

- predict future cash needs
- recommend deposit amounts
- adjust goals
- offer micro-savings nudges

- forecast balance health
- detect income volatility
- optimise savings habits

The savings account becomes a **financial copilot**.

7.2 Credit Cards Become Dynamic Credit Systems

Cards evolve from spending tools to intelligent liquidity systems:

- real-time, limit changes
- fraud prevention at the behavioural level
- dynamic interest rates
- micro-underwriting per transaction

7.3 SME Accounts Become Global Intelligence Hubs

SME banking becomes:

- cash flow-centric
- forecasting-driven
- multi-currency intelligent
- compliant automatically
- optimised for suppliers and vendors

7.4 Cross-Border Finance Becomes Frictionless

AI removes:

- complexity
- compliance bottlenecks
- friction
- risk

Customers receive:

- transparent pricing
- faster transfers
- personalised corridors

7.5 Lending Becomes a Behavioural Contract

A loan becomes:

- adaptive
- personalised
- self-adjusting
- predictive

The customer and bank enter a **dynamic agreement**, not a fixed contract.

8. The AI-Native Product Universe (Blueprint)

The AI-first bank eventually operates a unified product ecosystem that behaves like an organism.

Figure 3.7 – The AI-Native Product Universe

```
            +-------------------------+
            |    Identity Intelligence |
            | (Continuous Behavioural) |
            +------------+------------+
                         ↓
+-----------------------------------------------------------+
|                 Decision Intelligence Core                |
|  (Risk, Fraud, Credit, Pricing, AML, Compliance)          |
+------------+-------------------+--------------------------+
             ↓                   ↓
+------------------------+ +--------------------------+
| Lending Intelligence   | | Payments Intelligence    |
| Dynamic credit,        | | Routing, FX, fraud       |
| adaptive pricing       | | network detection        |
+------------------------+ +--------------------------+
             ↓                   ↓
+------------------------+ +--------------------------+
| SME/Business Systems   | | Treasury Intelligence    |
+------------------------+ +--------------------------+
```

Conclusion: AI-Native Products Are Not Digital Products with AI Embedded – They Are Entirely New Species

AI-native banking creates a **new product class**—dynamic, behaviour-driven, adaptive and continuously learning.

The bank does not deliver products.

The bank delivers **intelligent systems**.

This chapter established:

- How identity becomes behavioural
- How payments become predictive

- How credit becomes adaptive
- How fraud becomes network-aware
- How compliance becomes continuous
- How treasury becomes forward-looking
- How SME products become cashflow-driven
- How the entire product universe becomes intelligent

In Chapter Four, we will explore:

How to build an intelligence—first organisation: structure, culture, governance, model ops, and leadership.

"Intelligence is not a feature—it is the foundation on which the next century of financial institutions will be built."

CHAPTER 4

Building the AI-First Bank – Organisation, Governance, Leadership and Model Operations

"You cannot run an AI-first institution with a pre-AI organisation"

Most banks approach artificial intelligence as a technology initiative–something to be deployed, governed, and absorbed into existing structures. This chapter makes a different argument: AI does not transform banks because of better models or larger data sets, but because institutions are redesigned to allow intelligence to operate at scale. Building an AI-first bank requires a fundamental rethinking of organisation, governance, leadership, and operating models. Hierarchies must give way to decision networks, governance must evolve from static policy to continuous oversight, and leadership must shift from controlling processes to stewarding intelligence. Without these structural changes, AI remains trapped in pilots and proofs of concept. With them, intelligence becomes the bank's defining capability.

The failure of most AI initiatives in banking does not happen in the model – it happens in the organisation. Banks invest millions in data platforms, hire world-class data scientists, and pilot impressive proofs of concept, only to discover that intelligence stalls at the edge of legacy structures. Committees' slow decisions, governance frameworks are built for static systems, leadership treats AI as a technology programme, and operating models remain anchored to human-centric workflows. The uncomfortable truth is this: you cannot run an AI-first institution with a pre-AI organisation. Intelligence does not fail because models are weak – it fails because institutions are not built to let intelligence lead.

Digital transformation asked banks to upgrade technology.

AI transformation asks banks to **upgrade the institution itself**.

Digital demanded:

- channels
- apps
- automation
- cloud
- APIs
- journeys

AI demands:

- new teams
- New structures.
- New skills.
- New governance
- new ethical foundations.
- new operational rhythms.
- new decision rights.
- New leadership philosophies.

AI transformation is not a technology exercise; it is an **organisational re-architecture**. It changes who makes decisions, how decisions are made, how models are supervised, how risk is escalated, how teams collaborate, and how leaders manage uncertainty.

Digital banks looked modern.

AI-first banks think modern.

This chapter provides a full blueprint for:

1. AI-first organisational structure
2. Operating rhythms and workflows
3. Model operations (MLOps) and intelligence governance

4. Executive leadership and decision philosophy
5. Regulatory posture and model accountability
6. Talent architecture and cultural DNA

By the end of this chapter, you will have a clear map of what an AI-enabled financial institution looks like internally and how it works day to day.

1. AI Transformation Is an Org Challenge, Not a Tech Challenge

Banks often make the mistake of treating AI like:

- an IT initiative
- a data science project.
- a lab experiment.
- a vendor-driven upgrade.
- a pilot that must "prove itself"

This mindset guarantees failure.

AI is **not another tool**.

AI is a **new cognitive infrastructure**.

Just as the move to core banking changed everything in the 1980s...

Just as mobile banking changed everything in the 2010s...

AI changes the **entire operating system of the bank**.

When intelligence becomes the centre of the institution:

- decision-making centralises
- Teams reorganise.
- Governance modernises.
- Leadership shifts its mindset.
- Risk becomes algorithmic.
- Compliance becomes model-driven.

- Product becomes adaptive.
- Culture becomes experimental.

Technology cannot carry this transition alone.

Only the **institution** can.

2. The AI-First Organisational Structure

The AI-first bank has three new structural layers that traditional banks lack:

1. The Intelligence Organisation (IO)
2. The Decisioning and Orchestration Layer
3. Model Governance and Ethics Group (MGEG)

Let's break each down.

2.1 The Intelligence Organisation (IO)

This is the heart of the AI-first bank.

It owns the institution's intelligence assets.

The IO is composed of seven core teams:

1. **Data Engineering Team**

   Builds:

   - pipelines
   - ingestion flows.
   - streaming architecture.
   - lakehouses
   - feature stores.

2. **Machine Learning Engineers (MLEs)**

   Own:

- model deployment
- model optimisation
- Scaling Inference
- Latency management

3. **Data Science and Model Development Team**

   Build:

   - fraud models
   - Credit models.
   - risk models.
   - identity models.
   - Pricing models

4. **Intelligence Product Managers (IPMs)**

   Translate:

   - business needs
   - Model outputs.
   - decision goals.
   - confidence thresholds

5. **Model Monitoring and Risk Analytics**

   Track:

   - drift
   - anomalies
   - False positives
   - Model fatigue.
   - Precision/recall metrics.

6. **Behavioural Scientists and Economists**

   Interpret:

   - human behaviour
   - spending patterns,
   - Repayment dynamics
   - psychological friction.

7. **Decision Strategy Team**

   Tune:

   - approval strategy
   - Decline strategy.
   - Pricing elasticity.
   - Override rules.
   - escalation policies

(see Figure 4.1)

Figure 4.1 – The Intelligence Organization (IO)

```
          +----------------------+
          | Intelligence Org (IO)|
          +----------------------+
                 /      |      \
                /       |       \
+-------------+   +---+---+   +----------------+
| Data Eng    |   | MLEs  |   | Model Dev      |
+-------------+   +-------+   +----------------+
       \              |              /
        \             |             /
          +-----------+-------------+
                      |
        +-------------+-------------+
        | Intelligence Product Mgmt |
        +-------------+-------------+
                      |
        +-------------+-------------+
        | Model Monitoring & Risk   |
        +-------------+-------------+
                      |
        +-------------+-------------+
        | Behavioural Scientists    |
        +-------------+-------------+
                      |
        +-------------+-------------+
        | Decision Strategy Team    |
        +---------------------------+
```

2.2 The Decisioning and Orchestration Layer (DOL)

This is where intelligence meets policy.

The DOL manages:

- how model outputs turn into real decisions.
- limits
- approvals

- pricing
- Fraud-blocking
- AML escalation.
- KYB/KYC decisions.
- credit adjustments

The DOL ensures:

- Consistency.
- Transparency.
- fairness
- auditability
- regulatory compliance

It is the **central switchboard** of the AI-first bank.

2.3 Model Governance and Ethics Group (MGEG)

This is the regulatory backbone.

The MGEG owns:

- Explainability
- Transparency.
- fairness
- Bias testing.
- compliance
- reporting
- Approval for new models.
- override policies.

This team becomes as important as traditional compliance.

(see Figure 4.2)

Figure 4.2 – The Three AI-First Org Layers

```
+------------------------------------------------------------+
|              MODEL GOVERNANCE & ETHICS GROUP                |
| (Fairness, Bias, Explainability, Regulatory Compliance)    |
+-----------------------------+------------------------------+
                              ↓
+------------------------------------------------------------+
|           DECISIONING & ORCHESTRATION LAYER (DOL)           |
| (Policies, Overrides, Escalation, Approval Logic)           |
+-----------------------------+------------------------------+
                              ↓
+------------------------------------------------------------+
|              INTELLIGENCE ORGANIZATION (IO)                 |
| (Data, Models, Behaviour, Monitoring, Strategy)             |
+------------------------------------------------------------+
```

3. Model Operations (MLOps): The Engine Room of the AI-First Bank

MLOps is to AI-first banking what DevOps was to digital banking.

Without MLOps:

- models drift.
- Decisions degrade.
- False positives explode.
- Risk increases.
- Regulators intervene.
- Trust erodes.

MLOps ensures:

- Models are trained.
- Models are deployed.

- Models are monitored.
- Models are retrained.
- Models are governed,

3.1 The Five Loops of MLOps

1. **Data Loop**

   Where data is ingested, cleaned, enriched.

2. **Model Loop**

   Where models are trained, tested, validated.

3. **Deployment Loop**

   Where models are pushed to production.

4. **Monitoring Loop**

   Where drift, errors, bias and performance are tracked.

5. **Feedback Loop**

   Where customer behaviour re-feeds the model.

(see Figure 4.3)

Figure 4.3 – The Five Loops of MLOps

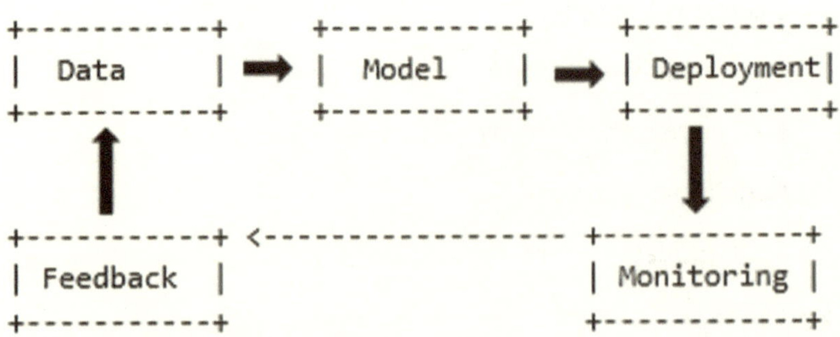

3.2 Model Drift: The Silent Killer

Models degrade for many reasons:

- customer behaviour changes.
- Economic shifts.
- merchant patterns evolve
- Fraud tactics change.
- Data channels expand.
- Seasonality impacts patterns.

Drift can:

- reduce accuracy
- increase false positives.
- distort pricing.
- weaken fraud defence.

In traditional banks, a broken model may go unnoticed for months.

In AI-first banks, drift is detected within hours.

3.3 Continuous Retraining

AI-first banks retrain models:

- weekly
- daily
- or continuously

Retraining can be:

- full
- Incremental.

- Triggered by drift,
- triggered by new signals,

Continuous retraining gives banks a dynamic intelligence advantage.

3.4 Human Oversight: Humans Must Stay in the Loop

AI-first banking requires:

- override committees
- Human-in-the-loop escalation.
- case managers
- model interpreters

AI does not replace humans.

AI augments humans.

4. Governance: The New Regulatory Architecture

Regulators will not ask:

"How many developers do you have?"

They will ask:

"How does your bank supervise its models?"

AI-first governance includes:

4.1 The Four Governance Pillars

1. **Explainability**
    - AI must be explainable to customers, regulators and internal teams.
2. **Fairness**
    - Models must be bias-tested and fair across demographics.

3. **Transparency**
    - Decisions must have an audit trail.
4. **Accountability**
    - Clear ownership of model outcomes.

4.2 Model Approval Standards

Every model must be approved based on:

- Performance.
- fairness
- stability
- robustness
- Explainability.
- Bias testing.

margin-left:36.0pt;text-align:justify;text-indent:-18.0pt;line-height:150%'>, regulatory compliance

4.3 Regulatory Alignment

AI-first banks align with:

- EU AI Act
- MAS FEAT. and Veritas
- FCA AI expectations.
- CBK, risk-based supervision
- OCC model risk standards.
- RBI's ML governance guidelines,

AI-first governance becomes a competitive advantage.

5. Leadership: The AI-First Executive Mindset

AI transformation requires a new kind of leadership philosophy.

Traditional banking leaders:

- rely on intuition
- use historical data
- trust committees
- Avoid experimentation
- move cautiously

AI-first leaders:

- rely on predictive data
- trust, experimentation
- Embrace uncertainty
- Delegate decisions to models
- adopt scientific thinking

5.1 The AI-First CEO

The AI-first CEO:

- treats intelligence as infrastructure
- fosters experimentation.
- builds cross-functional teams.
- demands model literacy.
- measures success by decision accuracy.

They do not ask,

"How fast is our app?"

They ask,

"How accurate are our decisions?"

5.2 The AI-First CRO

The CRO becomes:

- a model supervisor
- a drift monitor.
- a behavioural scientist.
- A data governance leader.

Risk becomes predictive.

5.3 The AI-First CTO / CDO

The technology leader becomes:

- a curator of signals
- a data ecosystem architect.
- an orchestrator of intelligence.
- , a guardian of model performance

5.4 The AI-First Product Leader

Product leaders:

- think in signals
- not in screens.
- Design for adaptation.
- Not for features.
- Manage feedback loops.
- not static journeys.

The product is not the interface.

The product is a **model-driven system**.

6. Culture: The DNA of the AI-First Bank

An AI-first culture has six fundamental traits:

6.1 Experimental Mindset

Every product, limit, model, and decision is a hypothesis that must be tested.

6.2 Evidence Over Ego

Data wins arguments.

Models win debates.

Evidence wins strategies.

6.3 Psychological Safety

People must feel safe challenging models, assumptions, and logic.

6.4 Speed of Decisioning

Weekly decisions

→ become daily decisions

→ become real-time decisions.

6.5 Interdisciplinary Collaboration

Risk, Compliance, Data, Product, and Engineering work as a single unit.

6.6 Ethical Integrity

AI must remain:

- fair
- equal

- Explainable.
- bias-free

Trust becomes the bank's #1 asset.

7. Operating Rhythms: How the AI-First Bank Works Daily

Daily rhythms shift from:

- status meetings,
- Steering committees
- Batch processes
- weekly reports

To:

- model monitoring
- drift checks
- Data pipeline health
- decision quality dashboards
- behavioural pattern alerts
- risk drift notifications

7.1 Daily

- Model performance review.
- Drift detection alerts.
- Fraud anomaly scan.
- Credit risk update.
- Treasury risk signals.
- Compliance monitoring.

7.2 Weekly

- Pricing model recalibration.
- Limit strategy updates.
- Behavioural segmentation refresh.
- Treasury forecasting adjustment

7.3 Monthly

- Model fairness testing.
- Regulatory reporting,
- Decision quality audit.
- Quarterly improvement roadmap.

8. AI-First Bank Maturity Model

Not all banks become AI-first overnight.

There are four maturity stages.

Stage 1: Model-Assisted Bank

- AI assists teams.
- Humans make decisions.
- Basic ML models deployed.

Stage 2: Model-Guided Bank

- AI recommends decisions.
- Humans override or approve.
- Decision orchestration begins.

Stage 3: Model-Led Bank

- AI automates 60–80% of decisions.
- human-in-the-loop for critical cases

Stage 4: Intelligence-First Bank

- decisions become real-time.
- Models operate continuously.
- Intelligence is the architecture.

(see Figure 4.4)

Figure 4.4 – The AI-First Maturity Curve

MODEL-ASSISTED → MODEL-GUIDED → MODEL-LED → INTELLIGENCE-FIRST
(Manual-heavy), (Hybrid), (AI-driven), (Fully adaptive)

9. AI-First Banks Operate as Living Systems

An AI-native bank:

- senses
- learns
- adapts
- predicts
- evolves
- self-corrects.

It resembles:

- an immune system (fraud defence)
- a brain (decision-making)
- a nervous system (signals),
- a circulatory system (data flows).

a digestive system (feedback loops),

The institution is no longer a rigid bureaucracy.

It is a **living intelligence organism**.

Conclusion: The Blueprint for the AI-First Bank

An AI-first bank is not a traditional bank with AI on top.

It is a **new species** of institution.

This chapter established:

- the Intelligence Organisation
- The Decisioning and Orchestration layer.
- The Model Governance and Ethics Group
- the MLOps engine.
- The leadership philosophy.
- The cultural DNA.
- the operating rhythms,
- the maturity curve

In the next chapter, we go beneath the org chart and into the bloodstream of the AI-first bank: the data strategy—how banks build, govern, and operationalise the intelligence pipeline that powers every model and every decision.

"AI does not transform banks when models get smarter. It transforms banks when institutions are redesigned to let intelligence lead."

CHAPTER 5

The Data Strategy of an AI-First Bank: How to Build, Govern and Exploit the Intelligence Pipeline

"If AI is the brain of the bank, data is its bloodstream."

Data is not a support function in an AI-first bank – it is the bank's strategic engine. This chapter explains how institutions build the intelligence pipeline that powers every real-time decision across credit, fraud, AML, pricing, onboarding, and treasury. We break down the end-to-end architecture of AI-ready data: what signals must be captured, how they are processed in real time, how features are engineered and governed, and how models consume them through decision orchestration. You will learn why most banks are "data-rich but signal-poor," how the signal advantage separates winners from laggards, and how governance, privacy, lineage, and feedback loops turn data into a durable competitive moat. By the end, you will have a practical blueprint to design a data-first institution capable of sustaining safe, explainable, and continuously improving intelligence at scale.

A fraud ring strikes at 2:17 a.m. – not with a brute-force attack, but with something more subtle: synthetic identities, clean-looking transactions, and behaviour engineered to resemble legitimate customers just closely enough to evade traditional controls. Within minutes, an AI-first bank detects an anomaly the human eye would never catch – not because it has better rules, but because its data pipelines are alive. Real-time signals stream in from devices, transactions, and networks; features update continuously; feedback loops sharpen the model's confidence. The bank intervenes before losses materialise, not through heroics or intuition, but through data architecture built for speed, lineage, and intelligence. In the next decade, the banks that win will not be the ones with the most data, but the ones that can transform raw signals into governed, real-time decisions. This chapter is about building that intelligence pipeline – the bloodstream of the AI-first bank.

If AI is the new brain of the bank, **data is its bloodstream**.

Every decision, every prediction, every fraud alert, every credit adjustment, every onboarding approval, every compliance escalation – every one of them depends on the quality, depth, granularity, and timeliness of data.

Banks often talk about AI as if it were magic.

But AI is not magic; AI is **math applied to data**.

A model is only as good as:

- the signals it receives.
- The features extracted.
- the data freshness.
- the data cleanliness,
- The feedback loops,
- The contextual intelligence.
- the behavioural richness

Traditional banks have massive amounts of data, but:

- Most of it is siloed.
- Much of it is unstructured.
- Some of it is incomplete.
- Most of it is stale.
- Nearly all of it is underutilised.

Digital transformation modernised data access.

AI transformation requires **data intelligence**.

This chapter explains:

1. The **four layers of AI-ready data**
2. How to build a **real-time data infrastructure**

3. How to govern data for **regulators, models, and decision engines**
4. The **types of data** AI-first banks must collect
5. The "**Signal Advantage**" and why it separates winners from losers
6. The role of **feature stores** and **data ontologies**
7. How data becomes the competitive moat of an intelligent institution

By the end, you will have a clear blueprint for a **true AI-ready data strategy**.

1. Why Data Is the New Balance Sheet

In traditional banking, value lives in:

- deposits
- loans
- assets
- branches
- customers

In AI-first banking, value lives in:

- signals
- features
- behaviour graphs.
- Identity data.
- risk attributes.
- Semantic networks

Money is no longer the only asset.

Data is an asset that generates intelligence, which generates better decisions, which generate profitability.

Banks that do not control their data pipelines will never control their decisions.

Banks that control their data pipelines will eventually control the entire value chain.

2. The Four Layers of AI-Ready Data

An AI-first data strategy has four distinct layers:

1. Data Collection Layer (Signals)
2. Data Processing Layer (Pipelines and Stream Engines)
3. Feature Layer (Feature Store and Feature Engineering)
4. Decision Layer (Model Inputs and Real-Time Orchestration)

You can think of these layers as the "data supply chain" of an AI-first institution.

(see Figure 5.1)

Figure 5.1 – The Four AI-Ready Data Layers

```
+----------------------------------------------------------+
|                 DECISION LAYER (MODELS)                  |
|       (Risk, Fraud, Credit, Pricing, Identity)           |
+----------------------------+-----------------------------+
                             |
+----------------------------------------------------------+
|             FEATURE LAYER (FEATURE STORE)                |
|     (Feature sets, behaviour features, derived signals)  |
+----------------------------+-----------------------------+
                             |
+----------------------------------------------------------+
|          DATA PROCESSING LAYER (STREAMS / ETL)           |
|     (Pipelines, transformations, real-time processors)   |
+----------------------------+-----------------------------+
                             |
+----------------------------------------------------------+
|               DATA COLLECTION LAYER (RAW)                |
|     (Transactions, device, behaviour, network, AML)      |
+----------------------------------------------------------+
```

3. The Data Collection Layer: The Raw Fuel of Intelligence

Banks historically collect:

- KYC documents,
- Basic demographics.
- Transaction logs.
- bureau scores.
- statements

This is foundational—but insufficient.

AI-first banks must collect **four categories of high-resolution data**:

3.1 Category 1 – Transactional Data (The Life Pattern Layer)

Transactional data reveals:

- spending patterns
- income rhythm
- financial behaviour
- financial stress signals
- repayment patterns
- spending entropy
- risk flags
- liquidity cycles
- earning stability

AI models depend heavily on transaction-level granularity.

Traditional banks summarise.

AI-first banks analyse **the raw sequence**.

3.2 Category 2 – Behavioural Data (The Identity Signal Layer)

Behavioural data includes:

- Typing cadence.
- Mouse movement.
- navigation flow.
- Device orientation.
- keystroke patterns.
- idle times
- retry patterns

These signals are:

- unique
- hard to spoof.
- real-time
- adaptive

They form a **behavioural fingerprint** that strengthens identity, fraud detection, and trust scoring.

3.3 Category 3 – Network Data (The Social and Economic Graph Layer)

Every customer is part of a network:

- employer
- beneficiaries
- merchants
- suppliers
- contacts
- devices

- IP addresses
- correlated identities

AI models use networks to:

- detect fraud
- score, SMEs
- Evaluate creditworthiness.
- Track risk propagation.
- Identify illicit clusters.

Network data is the new secret weapon.

3.4 Category 4 – External Data (The Contextual Layer)

This includes:

- bureau data
- social data
- geolocation
- business registration
- GST/VAT data
- sanctions lists
- fraud consortium data
- macroeconomic signals
- FX data
- news sentiment

AI-first institutions combine **internal** and **external** data to contextualise decisions.

4. The Data Processing Layer: Real-Time Pipelines and Stream Intelligence

Digital banks rely heavily on batch processing.

AI-first banks rely on **stream processing**.

Why?

Because intelligence must be:

- fresh
- real-time
- context-aware
- behaviourally sensitive

Batch data cannot power adaptive credit or predictive fraud.

Real-time data pipelines allow:

- instant limit adjustments
- real-time fraud detection
- continuous risk scoring
- adaptive onboarding
- dynamic pricing
- anomaly detection

4.1 Three Types of Data Pipelines

1. **Real-Time Stream Pipelines**

   For:

- fraud
- identity
- onboarding

- limit adjustments
- risk and credit decisions

2. **Near-Real-Time Pipelines**

   For:

   - segmentation
   - behavioural analysis
   - SME scoring
   - customer lifecycle intelligence

3. **Batch Pipelines**

   For:

   - reporting
   - historical modelling
   - regulatory submissions

AI-first banks operate all three in harmony.

(see Figure 5.2)

Figure 5.2 – Pipeline Types in AI-First Banking

REAL-TIME (ms–1s)

- Fraud decisioning
- Credit approvals
- Pricing adjustments
- Onboarding identity

NEAR-REAL-TIME (1–15 min)

- Behaviour segmentation
- SME scoring updates
- Limit recalibration

BATCH (Daily–Weekly)

- Historical models
- Regulatory reports
- Compliance summaries

5. The Feature Layer: The Brainstem of AI

Features are the **variables** models use to make decisions.

A traditional scorecard uses:

- 8-15 features

An AI-first model uses:

- **300–3,000+ behaviour features**

Examples:

- income entropy.
- Location variance.
- Repayment cadence.

- Device trust score.
- Merchant diversity.
- Transaction seasonality.
- risk velocity.
- network consistency.
- savings momentum.
- cash flow volatility

5.1 The Feature Store

A feature store is where:

- features live.
- features update.
- Features serve models.
- Features are versioned.
- Features are monitored.

It is the single most important database in any AI-first bank.

Without a feature store, AI models die.

(see Figure 5.3)

Figure 5.3 – The Role of the Feature Store

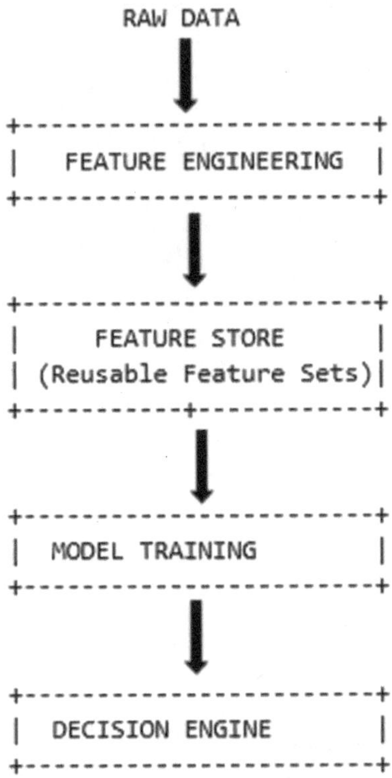

6. The Decision Layer: Where Data Becomes Intelligence

The Decision Layer takes:

- features
- signals
- probabilities.
- predictions

and converts them into:

- approvals
- declines

- escalations
- pricing adjustments
- limit changes
- onboarding pathways
- fraud blocks,
- Compliance alerts.

This is where **models become decisions**.

7. The 'Signal Advantage': The Real Competitive Moat

In traditional banking:

- Capital is the moat.
- Distribution is the moat.
- Trust is the moat.

In AI-first banking:

- **signals** are the moat.
- **behavioural intelligence** is the moat.
- **data richness** is the moat.

What is the "signal advantage"?

It is the ability to:

- Sense earlier.
- interpret better.
- Predict more accurately.
- respond more quickly
- personalise, deeper

The bank with the best intelligence wins.

Three Types of Signal Advantage

1. **Depth Advantage**

   How many behavioural layers you capture.

2. **Velocity Advantage**

   How fast you update the data.

3. **Context Advantage**

   How well you understand your customer's world.

(see Figure 5.4)

Figure 5.4 – The Three Signal Advantages

DEPTH (Granularity)

- Behavioural signals
- Device patterns
- Network graphs

VELOCITY (Speed)

- Real-time updates
- Continuous scoring
- Instant pipes

CONTEXT (Meaning)

- External data
- Macroeconomic factors
- Sentiment, intent

8. Data Governance: The Backbone of AI Integrity

Regulators now think in terms of:

- data lineage

- Data quality.
- Data fairness.
- Explainability.
- Purpose limitation.
- consent
- Retention policies.

AI-first banks must adopt **data governance frameworks** similar to those used in:

- healthcare
- telecom
- national security,

8.1 The Five Pillars of Data Governance

1. Quality
2. Lineage
3. Access Control
4. Privacy
5. Retention and Deletion

Pillar 1: Quality

Models cannot tolerate dirty data.

Pillar 2: Lineage

Every data point must be traceable.

Pillar 3: Access Control

Only the right teams should see the right data.

Pillar 4: Privacy

Consent, consent, consent.

Pillar 5: Retention

Only keep what is necessary for intelligence.

9. The Data Architecture of the AI-First Bank

AI-first banks use a **multi-zone data architecture**:

1. Raw Zone
2. Refined Zone
3. Feature Zone
4. Model Zone
5. Decision Zone

(see Figure 5.5)

Figure 5.5 – Multi-Zone Data Architecture

RAW ZONE

- Unprocessed data
- Full fidelity
- Time-stamped logs

REFINED ZONE

- Cleaned data
- Normalised
- Deduplicated

FEATURE ZONE

- Behavioural features
- Derived attributes

MODEL ZONE

- Training datasets
- Validation datasets

DECISION ZONE

- Real-time scoring
- Model execution
- Decision outputs

10. Data as an Organisational Muscle

Data strategy is not a tech strategy.

Data strategy is an **organisational muscle** that must be trained.

Every department must be:

- data-literate
- Signal-aware
- insights-driven

Risk teams must understand:

"What signals drive PD drift?"

Fraud teams must understand:

"How do network patterns propagate?"

Product teams must understand:

"What behavioural clusters are emerging?"

Leadership must understand:

"How does intelligence evolve?"

11. Feedback Loops: The Secret Weapon of AI-First Banks

The quality of an AI-first bank's decisions depends on the strength of its **feedback loops**.

Feedback includes:

- overrides
- False positives
- repayment behaviour,

- customer complaints.
- Transaction reversals.
- Fraud escalations.
- model errors.
- behavioural drift.

Banks that master feedback loops eventually overpower their competition.

Why?

Because:

- models improve faster.
- Risk declines.
- Customer experience improves.
- Fraud losses drop.
- approvals increase.

Feedback is how the institution learns.

(see Figure 5.6)

Figure 5.6 – The Feedback Intelligence Loop

Customer Behaviour

↓

Model Decision

↓

Outcome Observed

↓

Feedback Logged

↓

Model Retrained

12. Data Ethics and Responsibility

AI-first banks hold more behavioural data than ever before.

This creates responsibility:

- transparency.
- fairness
- Explainability.

-18.0pt;line-height:150%'>

- customer rights
- Opt-in systems

Ethics cannot be optional.

Ethics must be engineered into every pipeline.

13. The Data Maturity Model: From Digital to Intelligent

There are four maturity stages.

Stage 1 – Data-Aware

- Data exist
- No strategy
- Siloed

Stage 2 – Data-Enabled

- Pipelines exist
- Dashboards exist
- Limited ML

Stage 3 – Data-Intelligent

- Feature store

- Real-time scoring
- AI-driven decisions

Stage 4 – Data-First (AI-Native)

- Signals everywhere
- Continuous intelligence
- Fully adaptive decision engine

Figure 5.7 – Data Maturity Curve

DATA-AWARE → DATA-ENABLED → DATA-INTELLIGENT → DATA-FIRST

Conclusion: The Data Strategy Is the AI Strategy

There is no AI-first bank without a data-first institution.

This chapter established:

- the four data layers
- the pipeline architecture
- behavioural, network, and contextual signals
- feature stores
- governance models
- signal advantage
- feedback loops
- maturity curve

In Chapter Six, we explore **AI-first Risk, Fraud and Compliance**, and how intelligence reshapes the defensive backbone of banking.

"In the age of intelligent finance, the bank that controls its data pipelines controls its decisions, and the bank that controls its decisions controls its future."

CHAPTER 6

AI-First Risk, Fraud and Compliance: Rebuilding the Defensive Core of the Modern Bank

"In the AI era, risk is not managed after the fact. It is sensed, computed and neutralised in real time."

Risk, fraud, and compliance were designed for a slower, more predictable world—one where threats emerged gradually and controls could respond after the fact. This chapter shows how artificial intelligence rebuilds the defensive core of banking into a continuous, predictive intelligence system. It explains how behavioural data, network analysis, real-time scoring, and adaptive limits transform credit risk, fraud detection, AML, compliance, and security from siloed control functions into a unified, self-defending architecture. You will see why rules and periodic reviews fail in high-velocity environments, how AI enables risk to be sensed and neutralised in real time, and how governance evolves from checklists to model oversight. By the end of the chapter, risk is no longer something banks manage reactively—it becomes an always-on intelligence that protects the institution while enabling confident growth.

Risk is the silent engine of every financial institution.

Fraud is the ever-evolving enemy.

Compliance is the institutional conscience.

AML is the regulatory backbone.

Security is the fortress wall.

Model governance is the oversight system for the new age.

In the digital era, these functions were defined by:

- rules
- policies

- checklists
- periodic reviews
- document trails
- manual investigations
- spreadsheet analytics

Banks reacted to events.

They did not anticipate them.

The AI era flips this paradigm.

AI-first banks:

- predict risk
- anticipate fraud
- enforce compliance continuously
- evaluate identity perpetually
- detect networks behind transactions
- sense behavioural anomalies
- propagate risk insights across systems
- adapt limits in real-time
- monitor drift automatically
- generate alerts before damage occurs

In an AI-first institution,

risk becomes intelligence,

fraud becomes network analysis,

compliance becomes continuous,

security becomes behavioural,

AML becomes graph-based,

and **governance becomes model-centric**.

This chapter explains how.

1. Why Traditional Risk Architecture Cannot Survive the AI Era

Traditional risk frameworks were designed for:

- slower economies
- predictable behaviours
- domestic banking
- periodic data
- static identities
- hierarchical organisations
- batch processes

None of these assumptions holds anymore.

- customers behave dynamically
- fraudsters act globally
- markets shift rapidly
- creditworthiness evolves daily
- compliance expectations intensify
- regulators demand transparency
- data arrives in streams, not batches
- identity is no longer a document

Traditional risk frameworks break under this complexity.

1.1 The Four Cracks in Traditional Risk

A. Rules Cannot Adapt to Behavioural Change

Rules respond to the past.

AI responds to the present.

B. Manual Review Cannot Scale

Transaction volumes far exceed human capacity.

C. Static Models Lose Accuracy Quickly

Economic shocks, behavioural shifts, and fraud evolution outpace slow model refresh cycles.

D. Siloed Risk Teams Create Blind Spots

Fraud knows what credit does not.

Credit sees what AML does not.

AML detects what onboarding ignores.

AI-first risk solves these problems **at the root**, not at the symptom level.

2. The AI-First Risk Framework: Dynamic, Behavioural, Continuous

The AI-first risk framework has six capabilities:

1. **Behavioural Risk Modelling**
2. **Continuous Risk Scoring**
3. **Cashflow and Volatility Prediction**
4. **Macro-Sensitive Risk Adjustment**
5. **Network Risk Propagation**
6. **Adaptive Limits and Exposure Control**

The AI-first model is not a scorecard.

It is a **living risk organism.**

Figure 6.1 – The AI-First Risk Framework

```
+---------------------------+
|    Behavioural Signals    |
+-------------+-------------+
              ↓
+---------------------------+
|   Continuous Risk Model   |
| (Real-time PD & Risk Drift)|
+-------------+-------------+
              ↓
+---------------------------+
|  Exposure & Limit Engine  |
| (Adaptive Credit Controls) |
+-------------+-------------+
              ↓
+---------------------------+
| Risk Propagation Network  |
| (Cross-product, Cross-edge)|
+---------------------------+
```

3. Behavioural Risk: The New Foundation

Traditional risk relies on:

- static credit bureaus
- income statements
- repayment history
- demographic correlations

AI-first risk relies on **behaviour**.

3.1 Behaviour Patterns Are Stronger Predictors Than Credit Scores

A customer's probability of default is determined more by:

- cash flow patterns
- spending stability
- location consistency
- device trust score
- merchant relationships
- repayment rhythm
- volatility of earnings

than by:

- age
- gender
- job title
- education

3.2 Behavioural Risk Features Include:

- income entropy
- spending concentration
- frequency variance
- Inter-transaction intervals
- Salary consistency
- Irregular income shocks
- Bounce probability
- Savings momentum
- Risk velocity

These behavioural signals provide **real-time insight** into a customer's financial health.

4. Continuous Risk Scoring: From Static Ratings to Live Profiles

Traditional banks score risk:

- once during onboarding
- once during the loan application
- annually during review

AI-first banks score risk:

- every day
- every transaction
- every income inflow
- every behaviour change

If risk increases, limits shrink.

If risk decreases, capacity expands.

4.1 Risk Drift Detection

Risk drift happens when customer behaviour:

- changes suddenly
- becomes volatile
- becomes inconsistent
- deviates from historical norms

AI-first systems detect drift instantly.

Figure 6.2 – Continuous Risk Scoring Engine

Customer Behaviour Stream

↓

Feature Extraction

↓

Daily Risk Score Update

↓

Risk Drift Detector

↓

Exposure Adjustment

5. Cashflow Prediction and Income Volatility Modelling

AI-first lenders do not guess affordability.

They **predict** it.

Models evaluate:

- income cycles.
- earnings volatility
- probability of income drop
- seasonality
- sudden spikes or declines
- correlation with external conditions

5.1 Micro-SME Cashflow AI

For SMEs, cashflow patterns hold the truth.

AI models map:

- invoice cycles
- supplier payments
- customer concentration
- recurring subscription revenue
- inventory flows
- working capital strain

Risk becomes structural, not speculative.

6. Network Risk Propagation: Risk Spreads Like a Virus

A customer is not a standalone entity.

They exist within a **financial network**.

Examples:

- employees of the same employer
- merchants serving the same customers
- suppliers to the same SMEs
- users sharing devices
- transactions from the same location
- correlated beneficiaries

If one node becomes risky, the risk spreads across the network.

AI models detect this early.

Figure 6.3 – Network Risk Propagation

```
        Node A (High Risk)
                |
        +-------+---------+
        |                 |
Node B (Moderate)   Node C (Low)
```

AI Propagation:

Risk flows outward based on:

- Shared employer
- Shared device
- Correlated merchants
- Transaction timing

7. Adaptive Limits: Exposure Control in Real Time

Traditional limits:

- static
- inflexible
- reviewed manually

AI-native limits:

- adjust daily or weekly
- based on risk drift
- based on cash flow
- Based on network risk
- based on behaviour

If the customer becomes risky, limits shrink.

If the customer becomes stable, limits grow.

This reduces:

- loss rates
- portfolio volatility
- overexposure

8. AI-First Fraud Intelligence: From Rule Engines to Behaviour Graphs

Fraud evolves daily.

Rules evolve yearly.

This mismatch guarantees losses.

AI-first fraud systems:

- detect anomalies
- identify patterns
- predict attacks
- link criminals across networks
- escalate risk in milliseconds

Fraud is not a transaction-level event.

Fraud is a **network behaviour phenomenon**.

8.1 The Three Layers of AI Fraud Detection

1. **Behaviour Layer**
    - unusual spending
    - velocity escalation
    - device anomalies
2. **Network Layer**
    - shared merchants

- shared accounts
- shared devices
- shared beneficiaries
- IP fingerprint clusters

3. **Sequence Layer**
   - ordering of transactions
   - time-of-day patterns
   - switching behaviour

Figure 6.4 – Three Layers of AI Fraud Detection

BEHAVIOUR LAYER

- Unusual patterns
- Velocity anomalies

NETWORK LAYER

- Linked merchants
- Shared devices
- Beneficiary clusters

SEQUENCE LAYER

- Event ordering
- Time anomalies

8.2 AI Detects Fraud Faster Than Humans

- Rules detect known patterns.
- AI detects unknown patterns.
- Rules can be bypassed.
- Behaviours cannot be faked easily.

Fraudsters cannot hide their behavioural signatures.

9. AI-Driven AML and Compliance: Continuous, Graph-Based, Predictive

AML (Anti-Money Laundering) in traditional banks:

- retrospective
- manual
- checklist-based
- slow
- rule-driven

AI-first AML:

- continuous
- behaviour-driven.
- graph-based
- network-oriented
- predictive

9.1 AI Models Detect Suspicious Networks

AI identifies:

- layering
- structuring
- smurfing
- mule accounts
- funnel networks
- circular flows
- jurisdictional risk

AML becomes proactive.

Figure 6.5 – AML Graph Intelligence

```
User A --> User B --> Merchant X --> User C
   ↘          ↗
     +-------> Account Z ------+
 Suspicious loops, layering, clustering
```

9.2 KYB (Know Your Business) Becomes AI-Enhanced

KYB traditionally depends on:

- registration docs
- audited statements

But SMEs rarely have clean data.

AI uses:

- invoice networks
- POS device signals
- supplier graph
- cash flow rhythm
- repayment behaviour
- merchant risk

KYB becomes dynamic.

9.3 Sanctions and PEP Screening Becomes Real-Time

AI enhances:

- fuzzy matching
- language detection
- entity linking

- global watchlist scanning
- contextual weighting

False positives drop.

True positives increase.

10. AI-First Compliance: Compliance-as-Code

Compliance teams become intelligence teams.

Traditional compliance reviews:

- periodic
- manual
- form-driven

AI-first compliance:

- real-time
- continuous
- automated
- behaviour-based

Compliance becomes **embedded in the decision engine**.

Examples:

- transactions blocked based on model risk.
- onboarding flows adjusted for risk level.
- KYB strengthened for certain entities.
- PEP escalation automated.
- fraud checks integrated into AML logic.

Compliance becomes **programmatic**, Compliance-as-Code.

11. AI-First Security: Behavioural Security and Trust Scores

Security traditionally relies on:

- passwords
- OTPs
- tokens
- devices
- biometrics

AI-first security relies on:

- Behavioural biometrics
- Continuous authentication
- Device trust scores
- Risk-based session control
- Anomaly detection

11.1 Behavioural Biometrics Are Difficult to Fake

AI continuously analyses:

- hand pressure
- typing style
- scroll rhythm
- app navigation
- pinch/zoom patterns
- micro-movements

No fraudster can replicate all of these.

12. Decision Governance: The Most Important New Function

In the AI-first bank, governance shifts from:

- policies
- checklists
- procedures

to:

- model oversight
- drift monitoring
- fairness evaluation
- bias testing
- explainability

12.1 Model Governance Councils (MGCs)

MGCs approve:

- new models
- model updates
- retraining cycles
- drift thresholds
- override policies

MGCs track:

- false positives
- false negatives
- fairness gaps
- stability metrics
- calibration accuracy

13. The Role of the Human in an AI-First Defensive System

AI does not eliminate humans.

AI elevates humans.

Humans handle:

- complex cases
- ethical decisions
- disputed transactions
- edge cases
- regulatory explanations
- contextual risk

Models handle:

- volume
- velocity
- pattern detection
- probability estimation

The human and the model work together.

14. How AI Changes Every Defensive Unit

Credit Risk

Dynamic affordability

Cashflow forecasting

Behaviour signals

Fraud

Graph patterns

Anomaly detection

AML

Network intelligence

Continuous scanning

Compliance

Real-time controls

Programmatic interventions

Information Security

Behavioural defence

Continuous trust scoring

Operational Risk

Incident prediction

Root cause analytics

15. The Defensive Moat: AI Makes Banks Harder to Attack

AI-first banks become:

- harder to defraud
- harder to launder through
- harder to exploit
- harder to impersonate

Because:

- identity is continuous.
- fraud triggers are behavioural.
- AML checks are graph-based.
- risk is real-time.
- limits are adaptive.
- security is behavioural.

The AI-first bank is a **self-defending organism**.

Figure 6.6 – The AI-First Defensive Ecosystem

```
              +--------------------+
              |  Behavioural ID    |
              +---------+----------+
                        ↓
           +------------------------+
           |   Fraud Intelligence   |
           +------+-----------------+
                        ↓
      +----------------------------+
      |   Risk & Credit Models     |
      +-------------+--------------+
                        ↓
+---------------------------------------+
|        Compliance & AML Intelligence  |
+-------------+-------------------------+
                        ↓
             +---------------------+
             |   Decision Engine   |
             +---------------------+
```

16. The AI-First Regulatory Model of the Future

Regulators will begin asking:

- How do you explain your model?
- What are your bias-testing cycles?
- How do you track drift?
- Who approves retraining?
- What is your override impact?
- How are disclaimers communicated?
- Which features are used?
- What signals are included?

Banks must prepare for:

- AI audits
- model explainability reports
- algorithmic fairness reviews
- cross-border data lineage analysis

The regulator of the future supervises **models**, not just processes.

Conclusion: AI Rebuilds the Entire Defensive Core of Banking

AI-first banking introduces:

- behavioural risk
- continuous scoring
- adaptive limits
- network fraud detection
- graph-based AML
- compliance-as-code
- behavioural security
- model governance
- intelligence-driven operations

This chapter showed how AI rebuilds the entire defensive backbone of banking—credit, risk, fraud, AML, compliance, security, and governance into a single, adaptive intelligence system.

With the defensive core rebuilt, we now turn to the front of the institution. Chapter Seven explores how AI transforms customer experience, personalisation, and relationship banking, where intelligence becomes visible to the customer, not just the institution.

> **"In the age of intelligent finance, the safest banks are not the most controlled ones, but the most intelligent ones."**

CHAPTER 7

AI-First Customer Experience: Hyper-Personalisation, Relationship Intelligence and the New Frontline of Banking

"Digital made banking accessible. AI makes banking personal."

Screens, speed, or convenience no longer define customer experience—those are now table stakes. This chapter explores how AI transforms banking's frontline into an intelligence-driven relationship system that understands, anticipates, and adapts to each customer in real time. It shows how behavioural data, predictive models, and continuous learning enable hyper-personalisation across pricing, journeys, service, guidance, and engagement. You will see how AI reshapes relationship management, customer support, loyalty, and trust—moving experience from static journeys to living interactions. In the AI-first bank, customer experience is no longer designed once and delivered uniformly; it is learned continuously, personalised individually, and governed responsibly.

For the last decade, banks competed on:

- app design
- number of clicks
- onboarding speed
- journeys
- dashboards
- convenience

But convenience is no longer a differentiator.

Customers expect convenience as the baseline.

The next frontier is **intelligence-driven experience**—CX that

- understands the customer.
- anticipates needs.
- adapts to behaviour
- learns from patterns.
- personalises pricing.
- predicts financial stress.
- guides decisions.
- protects proactively.

An AI-first customer experience is not about "better UX."

It is about **relationship intelligence**.

Digital CX optimised screens.

AI CX optimises understanding.

This chapter explores how AI transforms:

1. Personalisation
2. Customer journeys
3. Service models
4. Relationship management
5. Financial guidance
6. Loyalty and engagement
7. Customer lifetime value
8. Customer support
9. Omni-channel orchestration
10. Customer trust

By the end, you will see that CX in an AI-first bank is not an interface; it is a behavioural intelligence system woven into every customer touchpoint.

1. The Evolution of Customer Experience in Banking

CX has evolved across four eras:

1. **Branch-Centric Experience** (pre-2005)
2. **Digital Experience** (2005–2015)
3. **Mobile-First Experience** (2015–2023)
4. **AI-First Intelligent Experience** (2023 onward)

Figure 7.1 – The Four Eras of Banking Experience

<u>BRANCH ERA</u>

• Human interaction
• Manual service
• Relationship managers

<u>DIGITAL ERA</u>

• Online banking
• Website portals
• Form workflows

<u>MOBILE ERA</u>

• App-centric
• 24/7 access
• Biometric login

<u>AI-FIRST ERA</u>

• Behaviour-driven experience
• Predictive personalisation
• Adaptive journeys
• Continuous guidance

2. The Three Engines of AI-First Customer Experience

AI-first CX is built on three engines:

1. **Personalisation Engine**
2. **Prediction Engine**
3. **Protection Engine**

These engines work together to create a banking experience that feels:

- tailored
- proactive
- empathetic
- intelligent

2.1 Engine One: Personalisation Engine

Traditional personalisation:

- "You might like this product."
- "Customers, like you, also bought..."
- Static segment-based offers

AI-native personalisation:

- behavioural micro-segmentation
- real-time product adjustments
- dynamic recommendations
- personalised pricing curves
- adaptive credit limits
- predictive nudges

Instead of placing customers into segments...

AI builds a **segment of one**.

2.2 Engine Two: Prediction Engine

AI predicts:

- risk.
- income volatility.
- spending trends.
- upcoming cash flow issues.
- likelihood of churn.
- ability to repay.
- life transitions.
- customer goals.

Prediction transforms CX from reactive to anticipatory.

2.3 Engine Three: Protection Engine

AI protects customers by:

- detecting fraud early.
- preventing scams.
- blocking suspicious transactions.
- alerting risky merchants.
- identifying account takeover attempts.
- predicting financial distress.

Protection becomes a form of customer experience.

Figure 7.2 – The Three Engines of AI CX

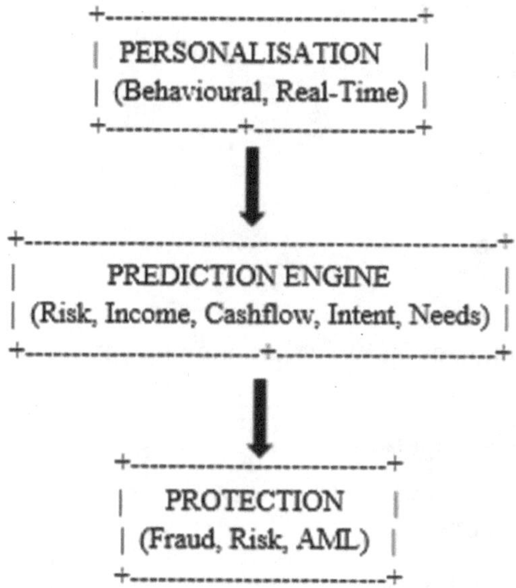

3. Hyper-Personalisation: Beyond Segmentation

Segmentation is a digital concept.

Hyper-personalisation is an AI-first concept.

3.1 Old Segmentation

- age
- gender
- income group
- job title
- geography

3.2 AI Hyper-Personalisation

- spending entropy

- behaviour clusters
- financial health score
- micro-risk profiles
- income volatility
- saving momentum
- liquidity resilience
- network stability

AI captures thousands of features that humans cannot.

Hyper-personalisation enables:

- tailored product offers
- personalised loan terms
- unique pricing curves.
- unique credit trajectories.
- individualised financial plans
- targeted nudges,
- customised risk shield

Customers don't want more features; they want a better fit.

4. Adaptive Customer Journeys: Journeys That Evolve in Real Time

In digital banks, journeys are predefined:

- 5-step onboarding
- 4-step loan application
- 7-step credit card activation
- fixed flows

In AI-first banks, journeys **adapt dynamically**.

If a customer:

- types slower → the form simplifies
- shows stress → prompts reduce
- shows confidence → advanced options appear
- wants speed → friction drops
- needs explanation → guidance increases

AI tunes:

- number of steps
- content
- flow
- options
- language complexity.

Customer journeys become **living flows**, not static templates.

Figure 7.3 – Static vs Adaptive Journeys

```
STATIC JOURNEY (DIGITAL)
Step 1 → Step 2 → Step 3 → Step 4 (same for everyone)

ADAPTIVE JOURNEY (AI-FIRST)
Step 1
 |
Behaviour Check
 |——→ Path A (expert user)
 |——→ Path B (needs help)
 |——→ Path C (high risk -> enhanced checks)
 |——→ Path D (low friction -> fast lane)
```

5. Financial Guidance: AI as the Customer's Financial Copilot

Customers rarely know:

- how much to save
- how much they can borrow.
- how to manage cash flow
- which product fits their needs.
- when they face liquidity challenges,

Banks traditionally provide:

- generic advice
- static brochures
- call centre scripts
- reminder notifications.

AI-first banks provide a **personal financial copilot**.

5.1 Predictive Financial Health Scoring

AI tracks:

- liquidity buffer
- cash flow volatility
- income consistency
- spending anomalies
- savings behaviours
- risk triggers

Customer receives:

- early warnings
- intelligent recommendations

- tailored nudges
- actionable insights

5.2 AI Anticipates Financial Stress

The bank warns the customer:

- 7–14 days before a cash shortage
- when bill payments will cause an overdraft
- when spending patterns become risky
- when credit usage is rising unsustainably

Human advisers cannot do this at scale.

AI can.

6. Dynamic Product Offers: Personalised Banking in Real Time

Products used to be **static**:

- fixed rates
- fixed terms
- fixed features
- fixed fees

AI makes products **adaptive**:

- changing credit terms
- dynamic fees
- personalised rewards
- tailored loan offers
- custom insurance bundles

Offers evolve with:

- behaviour

- needs
- goals
- life stages
- financial health
- risk profile

This creates customer loyalty through **precision fit**.

7. The AI-First Relationship Manager (RM): From Salesforce to Sentience

Relationship managers (RMs) traditionally rely on:

- notes
- spreadsheets
- CRM entries
- gut feel
- outdated dashboards

AI-first RMs have:

- behavioural insights
- predicted customer needs
- churn probability
- next best action guidance
- conversational intelligence

7.1 AI Becomes the RM's Copilot

AI tells RMs:

- whom to call
- when to call
- what to say

- what the customer needs
- which product fits
- which risk signals exist
- what life events may be upcoming

RMs become proactive, not reactive.

Figure 7.4 – AI-Augmented RM Workflow

Customer Behaviour Stream

↓

AI Insight Engine

↓

Next Best Action (NBA)

↓

RM Trigger (Call / Email / Push)

↓

Outcome Feedback

8. Customer Support Becomes AI-Augmented: Fast, Contextual, Emotional

Customer support is one of the biggest opportunities for AI.

Digital support is:

- scripted
- reactive
- slow
- inconsistent

AI-first support is:

- contextual

- predictive
- behaviour-aware
- empathetic
- automated
- consistent

8.1 Contextual Understanding

AI sees:

- what the customer was doing
- where they struggled
- what they clicked
- what failed
- their risk profile
- their behavioural signals

Support is instantly personalised.

8.2 Emotional Insight Through Sentiment Analysis

AI recognises:

- frustration
- confusion
- urgency
- hesitation
- satisfaction

Responses adjust tone accordingly.

9. Omni-Channel Intelligence: One Brain, All Channels

Digital banks unify channels.

AI-first banks unify **intelligence across channels.**

Customer can switch:

- chat → app → branch → IVR → RM

AI keeps the context intact.

9.1 One Customer Brain

Regardless of channel, AI knows:

- who you are
- what you need
- your risk level
- your product usage
- your behaviour path

The experience is seamless.

(see Figure 7.5)

Figure 7.5 – Omni-Channel Intelligence Architecture

```
APP ----\
CHAT ----> AI CUSTOMER BRAIN ----> RM DESKTOP
WEB ----/
BRANCH /
IVR   /
```

All channels share:

- Context
- Risk
- Behaviour
- Identity

- Preferences
- Predictions

10. Loyalty and Engagement: From Rewards to Relevance

Loyalty today is:

- cashback
- reward points
- discounts
- promotions

These do not build emotional loyalty.

They build transactional loyalty.

AI builds:

- loyalty through confidence
- loyalty through personalisation
- loyalty through protection
- loyalty through relevance

When a bank anticipates your needs, you stay.

When a bank protects you silently, you trust.

When a bank reduces your stress, you commit.

11. Customer Lifetime Value (CLV): AI Turns CLV Into a Living Metric

Banks traditionally compute CLV:

- quarterly
- through static formulas

AI computes CLV:

- daily

- dynamically
- behaviourally

11.1 AI Predicts CLV Changes

Signals include:

- product adoption
- earnings growth
- income consistency
- savings acceleration
- churn risk
- cross-product affinity

With this intelligence:

- Marketing becomes precise.
- Product offers become relevant.
- Rm engagement becomes targeted.

12. Churn Prediction: Preventing Customer Loss Before It Happens

Customers rarely leave suddenly.

Churn follows:

- declining engagement
- increased friction
- rising dissatisfaction
- risky behaviour
- cashflow stress
- competitive pressure

AI identifies churn **weeks before it occurs**.

12.1 AI Evaluates 60+ Churn Signals

Including:

- login frequency
- product usage
- transaction patterns
- device behaviour
- app drop-off points
- complaint frequency
- failed payments
- fund flows to competitors

Interventions become:

- timely
- tailored
- contextual

13. Trust, Transparency, and Ethics: AI as the Foundation of Relationship Banking

AI-first banks must be:

- transparent
- explainable
- fair
- privacy-respecting

Trust is the currency of customer experience.

Customers ask:

- Why was my price adjusted?

- Why did my limit change?
- How does the bank use my data?
- How is my risk evaluated?

AI cannot be a black box.

AI must be a **glass box**.

14. The AI Customer Experience Maturity Model

There are four maturity stages.

Stage 1 – Digital Personalisation

- static segments
- simple offers
- basic recommendations

Stage 2 – Behavioural Personalisation

- behavioural clusters
- context-aware offers

Stage 3 – Predictive Personalisation

- nudges
- risk prediction
- income forecasting

Stage 4 – Autonomous Experience Engine

- AI adapts journeys
- AI personalises pricing
- AI predicts needs
- AI shields risk
- AI guides financial behaviour

Figure 7.6 – AI CX Maturity Curve

DIGITAL → BEHAVIOURAL → PREDICTIVE → AUTONOMOUS

Conclusion: AI Customer Experience Is Not a Luxury – It Is the New Competitive Standard

This chapter established that AI-first CX is built on:

- hyper-personalisation
- adaptive journeys
- predictive guidance
- behavioural intelligence
- omni-channel awareness
- continuous protection
- RM augmentation
- financial copilots
- trust and explainability

The future belongs to banks that:

- anticipate
- personalise
- protect
- guide
- understand

As customer experience becomes intelligent, adaptive, and personal, the implications extend far beyond retail interactions. The same intelligence that understands individual behaviour can be applied to businesses, supply chains, and the real economy at scale. In Chapter Eight, we move from the customer-facing frontline to the engine room of growth, exploring how AI rewires SME and business banking, where complexity is higher, margins are deeper, and the economic impact is greatest.

"In the AI era, customer experience is no longer designed – it is learned."

CHAPTER 8

AI-First Business and SME Banking: Rewiring Credit, Cashflow, Trade, and Treasury for the Real Economy

"The future of banking will be decided where money meets the real economy."

Business and SME banking sits at the heart of the real economy, and yet it remains one of the least modernised areas of financial services. This chapter explores how AI rewires business banking from the ground up, transforming credit underwriting, working capital, trade finance, cash management, FX, and treasury into continuous, intelligence-driven systems. It shows how behavioural data, transaction flows, platform signals, and network intelligence allow banks to underwrite businesses dynamically rather than relying on static documents and delayed financials. You will see how AI turns banks into proactive financial partners for SMEs—predicting cashflow stress, optimising liquidity, strengthening supply chains, and enabling sustainable growth. In the AI-first bank, business banking is no longer about processing files; it is about financing the real economy with precision, speed, and intelligence.

Small- and medium-sized businesses are the engines of the economy, but for decades, banks have tried to finance them using tools designed for a slower, simpler world. Credit decisions depend on outdated financial statements, working capital lines remain rigid, trade finance is buried under paperwork, and treasury services are reserved for large corporates. Meanwhile, the reality of SME life is dynamic, volatile, and deeply data-rich. Every transaction, invoice, payroll run, and supplier payment tells a story about cashflow, resilience, and risk. In an AI-first bank, that story is no longer ignored. Intelligence replaces paperwork. Behaviour replaces collateral. And business banking evolves from manual underwriting into a living system that learns, adapts, and grows alongside the real economy.

"Retail banking made digital headlines.

But SME and business banking will be where AI creates real economic value."

Most banks publicly talk about digital innovation in retail:

- mobile apps
- personal loans
- credit cards
- wallets
- super apps

But **the real engine of profitability and impact sits in business and SME banking**:

- working capital
- trade finance
- merchant services
- cash management
- FX and hedging
- term loans and asset finance
- supply chain finance
- treasury services

Yet this high-value segment is often the **least modernised**.

SMEs still:

- submit PDFs and Excel files
- upload bank statements manually
- face slow and opaque approvals
- endure rigid collateral requirements
- struggle with foreign payments
- get generic products, not built for their volatility

Banks still:

- use basic financial ratios
- rely on static balance sheets
- manually review statements
- use local bureaus with patchy data
- treat SMEs as "small corporates" or "big retail"

Digital transformation gave SMEs:

- online portals
- internet banking
- mobile access

But it **did not change the logic of SME and business banking**.

AI does.

AI for SMEs is not about putting a slick interface on old products.

It is about **re-underwriting the real economy**, using data.

This chapter explains how AI:

1. Rebuilds SME credit
2. Transforms working capital and invoice finance
3. Reimagines trade finance and supply chains
4. Reinvents business payments and cash management
5. Activates FX and treasury intelligence for SMEs
6. Defines the architecture of AI-first SME banking

1. Why SME Banking Has Been Broken for Decades

SME banking has always sat in a blind spot:

- too small for full corporate banking
- too complex for retail-style automation

SMEs are:

- volatile
- seasonal
- informal in many markets
- thin file in bureaus
- dependent on a few large buyers or suppliers
- often mixed with the founder's personal accounts

Traditional underwriting struggles with this complexity.

1.1 The Old SME Credit Model

Banks typically rely on:

- audited financials (often delayed or weak)
- collateral valuation
- static ratios (DSCR, leverage, coverage)
- vintage tax returns
- basic sector-level risk

This model is:

- slow
- manual
- biased towards older, formal SMEs
- blind to dynamic businesses
- poorly suited for digital-first or platform-based SMEs

1.2 The Result

- Good SMEs are rejected or underfunded
- Risky SMEs slip through heuristics

- Turnaround times are long
- Bankers avoid the segment or overprice it
- Fintechs and alternative lenders step in

SME banking, in most markets, is **under-lent and underserved**.

2. AI Rebuilds the SME Credit Brain

AI brings one fundamental shift:

Instead of underwriting documents, AI underwrites behaviour.

SMEs leave rich data trails:

- bank transaction flows
- POS/merchant acquirer data
- platform data (e-commerce, ride-hailing, logistics)
- payroll and staff patterns
- invoicing systems
- ERP, accounting, and inventory tools
- tax filing systems (GST/VAT)

2.1 Behavioural and Transactional Credit Models

AI-first SME models ingest:

- credits and debits over time
- seasonality of revenue
- concentration of customers
- supplier dependencies
- payment delays to vendors
- payroll regularity
- cashflow gaps and their duration

- frequency of overdrafts
- bounced payments
- inventory purchases vs sales

Instead of a static snapshot, AI builds a **dynamic financial portrait**.

Figure 8.1 – From Document-Centric to Behaviour-Centric SME Credit

DOCUMENT-CENTRIC (OLD)

Inputs:

- Audited financials
- Tax returns
- Collateral valuation

Output:

- One-time credit decision
- Static limit
- Fixed tenure

BEHAVIOUR-CENTRIC (AI-FIRST)

Inputs:

- Bank transaction flows
- POS/sales data
- Invoice networks
- Payroll patterns
- Tax filings (live)
- Platform data (e-com, logistics)

Output:

- Dynamic risk score
- Adaptive limit
- Flexible structures
- Early-warning signals

2.2 Invisible SMEs Become Bankable

Many SMEs previously considered "unbankable":

- informal
- thin file
- platform-native
- cash flow-based

become **bankable** because:

- AI reads their platform data.
- AI understands their transaction flows.
- AI maps their network relationships.

Ride-hailing drivers, small online sellers, micro-logistics shops, freelance collectives, and service providers can all be evaluated through **behaviour rather than collateral**.

3. Working Capital and Invoice Finance: AI as the Supply Chain Radar

Working capital is the lifeblood of SMEs.

Traditional working capital lending:

- depends on collateral.
- uses rigid limits.
- ignores real-time invoice data.
- treats all invoices equally.

This creates inefficiencies:

- SMEs struggle to meet payroll and pay suppliers.
- Delays in buyer payments cause liquidity gaps.
- Credit lines are either too low or too high.
- Risk is managed crudely.

AI changes this completely.

3.1 Invoice-Level Risk Intelligence

AI can evaluate risk **per invoice**, not per borrower.

Inputs:

- buyer behaviour
- invoice history
- payment timelines
- dispute frequency
- sector volatility
- macro conditions

AI computes:

- probability that the invoice will be paid
- expected payment date
- cashflow forecasting

The bank can then:

- finance selected invoices
- adjust advance rates dynamically
- price risk per buyer, per invoice, per tenor

Figure 8.2 – AI-Powered Invoice Risk Model

Invoice Attributes:

- Buyer risk score
- Historical payment behaviour
- Invoice amount and tenor
- Sector risk
- Counterparty network

AI Model Output:

- Probability of Payment (PP)
- Expected Payment Date (EPD)
- Recommended Advance %
- Risk-based Pricing

3.2 Dynamic Working Capital Lines

Instead of a fixed limit:

- AI adjusts the working capital limit in line with revenue patterns.
- SMEs with rising, stable cash flows get increased capacity.
- SMEs under stress get early-warning flags and structured support.

This creates a **symbiotic relationship** between the bank and SME.

4. Trade Finance and Supply Chain Finance: From Paper to Predictive Intelligence

Trade finance remains one of the most paper-heavy, manual, and friction-filled areas in banking.

Letters of credit, guarantees, collections, open account trade, documentary credits—all involve:

- manually checked documents
- limited visibility
- siloed risk assessments
- poor fraud detection

4.1 AI in Trade Documentation and Compliance

AI can:

- read trade documents (invoices, BLs, packing lists);

- detect inconsistencies;
- match shipment data to invoices;
- detect potential fraud or over/under-invoicing;
- identify dual-use or sanctioned goods;
- cross-check against trade-based money laundering typologies.

This dramatically reduces:

- manual workload
- processing time
- compliance risk

4.2 Supply Chain Networks as Risk Intelligence Graphs

Traditionally, banks saw:

- the direct client (the SME or corporate)
- some knowledge of their main suppliers or buyers

AI sees:

the entire **network** – multiple tiers deep.

Figure 8.3 – AI-Enhanced Supply Chain Graph

```
Tier 2 Supplier A ----> Tier 1 Supplier X ----> SME Customer ----> Buyer M
       \                 \
        \                 ---> Buyer N
         \
         ---> Tier 1 Supplier Y ----> SME Customer (Other line)
```

AI tracks:

- Risk across the network
- Dependency on key nodes
- Counterparty fragility
- Payment behaviours along the chain

AI models detect:

- over-dependence on a single buyer
- systemic risk from a vulnerable supplier
- concentration risk in a specific geography
- early signs of supply chain breakdown

Banks can use this to:

- adjust exposure
- recommend diversification
- structure better trade facilities
- create tiered financing (supplier finance, dealer finance, distributor finance)

5. Business Payments, Cash Management, and Collections: AI as the CFO's Sidekick

Larger SMEs and mid-market businesses rely heavily on:

- payments
- collections
- reconciliation
- payroll
- FX
- liquidity management

Banks offer:

- cash management platforms
- corporate internet banking
- host-to-host connections

But many still lack **intelligence**.

AI fills that gap.

5.1 Smart Collections and Receivables Intelligence

AI:

- identifies which customers are slowing payments
- predicts which invoices will default or delay
- suggests proactive collection steps
- segments customers by behaviour (reliable, volatile, risky)

SMEs gain:

- visibility into receivables health
- prioritisation for follow-up
- structured collection strategy

Banks gain:

- better view of borrower stress
- early warning on portfolio risk

5.2 Payment Optimisation and Cost Intelligence

AI can:

- recommend optimal timing for payments
- minimise interest cost
- balance between early payment discounts and liquidity needs
- optimise use of credit lines
- predict future obligations

The SME dashboard evolves from:

"This is your balance and these are your transactions."

to:

"Here's how to schedule payments this week to preserve cash, maintain supplier trust, and minimise fees and interest."

5.3 AI-Driven Liquidity Assistance

For SMEs with multiple accounts, currencies and facilities, AI can:

- suggest internal transfers
- optimise use of overdrafts vs term loans
- recommend cash pooling
- forecast liquidity squeezes
- alert to idle cash that can be invested

The bank becomes a **virtual CFO** for the SME.

Figure 8.4 – AI as SME Liquidity Copilot

Inputs:

- Incoming invoices
- Outgoing bills
- Payroll schedule
- Tax obligations
- Credit line limits

AI Output:

- Cashflow forecast
- Suggested payment schedule
- Recommended credit line draw
- Risk alerts (shortfall, overdraft)

6. FX, Hedging and Treasury for SMEs: Democratising Sophisticated Tools

Most SMEs are exposed to FX risk, but:

- they don't fully understand it
- they cannot access sophisticated tools
- products are too complex or expensive

AI helps:

- quantify exposure
- simulate scenarios
- recommend hedging strategies
- simplify complex instruments into intuitive recommendations

6.1 AI Quantifies FX Risk for SMEs

AI examines:

- recurring import payments
- export receipts
- cross-border payroll
- platform charges in foreign currency
- loans denominated in FX

Models:

- estimate FX-at-risk
- predict worst-case scenarios
- alert to concentration risk

6.2 Simple Recommendations, Complex Intelligence

Instead of jargon:

- "You have a 30–40% probability of FX-related cash flow stress over the next 90 days if the currency moves against you by 8–10%. We recommend hedging X% of your exposure using Y product on Z timeline."

Complex math. Simple communication.

7. SME Product Design: AI-Native Business Banking Products

AI-first SME banking is not about:

- repackaging retail loans for SMEs
- simply adjusting ticket sizes

It is about **inventing new product classes**:

1. Dynamic working capital lines
2. Invoice-level financing
3. Revenue-based lending
4. Platform-connected lending (POS, e-com, delivery apps)
5. Embedded finance for SMEs
6. Cashflow-backed term loans
7. AI-curated trade finance bundles

7.1 Revenue-Based Lending

AI-based models:

- tie repayment to revenue
- scales monthly repayment up or down
- manage risk through real-time monitoring

Great for:

- seasonal businesses
- digital merchants
- subscription-based SMEs

7.2 Embedded SME Credit in Platforms

SMEs operating on:

- marketplaces
- delivery apps
- social commerce platforms

can:

- receive embedded credit based on platform data
- get paid faster through financing
- manage working capital inside the platform

This requires:

- APIs
- continuous risk evaluation
- joint risk frameworks

AI runs this in the background.

8. The Architecture of AI-First SME and Business Banking

Combining the elements from previous chapters, the AI-first SME architecture looks like this:

Figure 8.5 – AI-First SME Banking Architecture

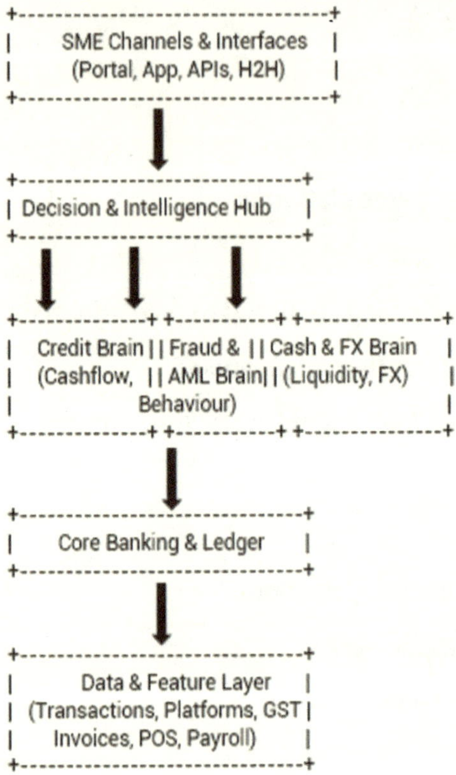

9. Relationship Managers and AI: Business Banking 2.0

In SME and business banking, relationship managers (RMs) are still crucial:

- trust
- negotiation
- complex structuring
- advisory

AI does not replace RMs—it **augments** them.

9.1 AI-Enhanced RM Capabilities

AI provides:

- client risk snapshots
- upcoming cash issues
- portfolio early-warning signals
- suggested proposals
- cross-sell opportunities
- churn risk
- client news and sentiment

RMs receive:

- prioritised call lists
- tailored talking points
- AI-generated proposal drafts
- alerts for important client events

This transforms RM banking from reactive firefighting to proactive partnership.

Figure 8.6 – AI-Augmented RM Dashboard

RM DASHBOARD:

Client: ABC Traders

- Risk: Stable (last 90 days)
- Cashflow: Tight next 14 days
- Opportunity: Invoice Finance on Buyer X
- Recommendation: Offer WC Top-up + FX advisory
- Alert: Buyer Y delaying payments (30 days avg delay).

10. AI and Business Banking Culture: From "File Pushers" to Strategic Partners

In many banks, SME/business units are stuck in:

- file pushing
- credit committee queues
- documentation management
- firefighting collections.

AI frees human capacity.

Back-office time moves to:

- advisory
- structuring
- problem solving
- ecosystem building

Business bankers can:

- design industry-specific solutions
- build ecosystem partnerships
- co-create financial products with platforms
- provide sectoral insights

AI takes away repetitive judgement.

People focus on strategic judgement.

11. Risk, Compliance, and AI in SME Banking

Earlier chapters covered AI-first risk and compliance.

In the SME and business context, this becomes especially powerful:

- AI detects suspicious trade-based money laundering structures.

- AI flags shell companies and high-risk beneficial ownership patterns.
- AI tracks unusual cross-border flows.
- AI evaluates fake invoicing networks.
- AI spots collusive fraud between SMEs and counterparties.

SME portfolios are historically considered risky due to opacity.

AI brings **transparency and granularity**.

12. Small Corporations and Mid-Market: The Sweet Spot for AI Value

Large corporations already have:

- sophisticated treasury
- multiple banking relationships
- strong financial discipline

Micro-businesses have:

- platform-based offers
- basic digital tools

The **mid-market and upper SME segment** sits in between, often underserved.

AI:

- processes their complexity
- recognises their patterns
- helps structure tailored facilities
- supports risk-adjusted growth

This segment becomes:

- the most profitable part of the bank's book
- the most strategically important

13. The SME and Business Banking AI Maturity Curve

We can define SME AI maturity in four stages.

Stage 1 – Digitally-Enabled SME Banking

- online portals
- scanned documents
- basic lending

Stage 2 – Data-Assisted SME Credit

- financial spreading tools
- sector scoring
- limited digital decision-making

Stage 3 – Behavioural AI SME Banking

- transaction-based models
- dynamic limits
- AI credit engines

Stage 4 – Fully AI-Native SME Banking

- embedded finance
- real-time risk
- cash flow copilots
- network-aware pricing
- trade graph intelligence

Figure 8.7 – SME and Business Banking AI Maturity

DIGITAL → DATA-ASSISTED → BEHAVIOURAL → AI-NATIVE

14. The Strategic Prize: Why AI-First SME and Business Banking Matters

Why does this matter so much?

Because SMEs:

- drive GDP
- employ the majority of workers
- define local economic resilience
- fuel innovation

And yet, they have always lived in a risk "fog."

AI clears that fog.

For banks:

- lower NPLs
- better RWA efficiency
- deeper cross-sell
- higher fee income
- more resilient books

For SMEs:

- fairer access
- faster decisions
- better product-market fit
- more sustainable growth

For economies:

- stronger employment
- healthier supply chains
- more inclusive growth

AI-first SME and business banking is not a technology project.

It is a **national economic upgrade**.

Conclusion: AI Returns Banking to Its Real Purpose – Financing the Real Economy

Retail banking gets the headlines.

Business banking moves the economy.

This chapter has shown how AI:

- rebuilds SME credit using behaviour
- transforms working capital and invoice finance
- makes trade and supply chain finance more transparent
- gives SMEs access to CFO-like intelligence
- democratises FX and treasury insights
- augments RMs with real-time intelligence
- strengthens risk and compliance in complex portfolios

In Chapter Nine, we will go deeper into **AI, Platforms and Embedded Finance**—how distribution shifts from acquiring customers to embedding intelligence inside the ecosystems where customers already live and work.

"The real economy doesn't need more paperwork. It needs better intelligence."

CHAPTER 9

AI, Platforms and Embedded Finance: The New Distribution Architecture of Intelligent Banking

"Finance wins when it disappears into the customer's life."

Embedded finance is the mechanism. Invisible finance is the outcome. Platforms are the distribution layer, and AI is what makes it scalable, safe, and profitable. This chapter explores the evolution of finance as it dissolves into everyday experiences through APIs, platforms, ecosystems, and partnerships. It explains why the future of financial services is not banking-as-a-destination but banking-as-an-invisible-layer embedded in commerce, mobility, lifestyle, and enterprise flows. Finance becomes most powerful when it disappears into context.

You don't wake up wanting to "do banking" – you wake up wanting to buy, move, travel, trade, earn, or build. Finance becomes powerful when it blends into these moments, invisible yet omnipresent. Walk into a car showroom, and financing appears instantly. Pay a supplier, and working capital flows seamlessly. Step into an online marketplace, and the bank is already there. Finance stops being a destination and becomes an integrated layer of life.

"Banks used to own the customer.

Then platforms owned the customer.

Now, AI decides who wins the customer."

For decades, banks distributed products directly:

- branch
- RM
- website
- mobile app

Digital transformation expanded distribution:

- APIs
- online onboarding
- partner portals

But starting 2021–2025, a new model emerged:

- platforms
- marketplaces
- gig networks
- e-commerce ecosystems
- mobility apps
- logistics platforms
- social commerce infrastructure

These platforms do not compete with banks for deposits.

They compete for **customer engagement**, the new battleground of banking.

In the AI era, value shifts from:

- ownership → to access
- products → to intelligence
- branches → to ecosystems
- direct distribution → to embedded distribution.
- customer acquisition → to customer activation
- core banking → to contextual banking

This chapter explains how AI, platforms, and embedded finance reshape:

1. Distribution
2. Product delivery
3. Credit

4. Payments
5. Trade
6. Risk
7. Business models
8. Regulation
9. Competitive moats

And how banks can survive and thrive in this new system.

1. The Shift to Platform Economy Is Irreversible

Today, consumers don't live inside banks.

They live inside **platforms**:

- Uber
- M-Pesa
- Shopify
- TikTok
- Amazon
- Jumia
- MercadoLibre
- Gojek
- Grab
- Bolt
- Careem
- Flutterwave

Businesses don't live inside banks either.

They live inside:

- ERP systems
- marketplaces
- procurement platforms
- logistics networks

Banks still think:

"How do we bring customers into our ecosystem?"

Platforms think:

"How do we embed financial intelligence into our ecosystem?"

AI accelerates this.

2. Understanding the Platform Advantage

Platforms have three structural advantages over banks:

2.1 Advantage 1: Daily Engagement

Banks see customers:

- weekly
- monthly
- rarely

Platforms see customers:

- every day
- every hour
- every transaction
- every behaviour

This produces rich behavioural data.

2.2 Advantage 2: Contextual Relevance

Platforms know:

- what customers buy
- where they spend
- when they travel
- how they earn
- what they search

Banks typically know:

- balances
- transactions

But not **intent**.

2.3 Advantage 3: Distribution at Scale

Platforms aggregate:

- audiences
- merchants
- employees
- gig workers
- SMEs

Banks spend billions acquiring customers.

Platforms do it through natural demand.

3. The AI Revolution: Why Platforms Become Financial Powerhouses

Platforms use AI for:

- ranking

- recommendations
- pricing
- fraud detection
- user retention
- search optimisation

This AI infrastructure becomes the foundation for:

- credit
- payments
- insurance
- risk
- onboarding

Platforms already think like AI-first banks.

Figure 9.1 – Platform AI vs Bank AI (Starting Advantage)

PLATFORMS:

- Daily behaviour data
- Deep engagement loops
- Rich context
- High-frequency transactions
- Unified user identity across actions

BANKS:

- Financial transaction data
- Periodic engagement
- Narrow context
- Lower frequency actions
- Fragmented identity systems

Platforms do not want to become banks.

But they want to **distribute financial services intelligently**.

Banks do not want to lose customers.

But they lack AI-native distribution models.

The solution is **embedded finance**.

4. The Embedded Finance Model: Banking Outside the Bank

Embedded finance places banking inside:

- ride-hailing apps
- e-commerce checkouts
- SaaS platforms
- payroll systems
- supplier networks
- gig worker apps
- freelancer platforms
- developer ecosystems
- travel apps

Instead of customers coming to the bank...

The bank comes to the customer.

4.1 Embedded Finance Includes

Payments

- payment rails inside apps
- checkout services
- instant payouts

Credit

- BNPL
- revenue-based lending
- inventory finance
- cashflow-based limits

Insurance

- ride insurance
- shipment protection
- product warranties

Accounts

- wallet
- virtual accounts
- sub-accounts

Identity

- KYC/KYB via platform data
- behavioural biometrics

FX

- cross-border flows
- dynamic FX pricing

Everything becomes **contextual**.

Figure 9.2 – Embedded Finance Examples

E-COMMERCE PLATFORM:

- BNPL at checkout
- Merchant working capital
- Cross-border FX

GIG PLATFORM:

- Instant payouts
- Daily-float credit
- Fuel loans

LOGISTICS PLATFORM:

- Invoice finance
- Shipment insurance
- Duty/tax payments

5. The Intelligence Layer: Why AI Makes Embedded Finance Explosive

AI enhances embedded finance in four ways:

5.1 Intelligence 1 – Platform Data Creates Better Credit Models

Platform data includes:

- ratings
- cancellations
- order volume
- dispute frequency
- delivery times
- customer satisfaction

These signals correlate strongly with risk.

AI models combine:

- bank data
- platform data
- behaviour data
- network data

Credit decisions become:

- real-time
- granular
- dynamic
- personalised

5.2 Intelligence 2 – AI Enables Real-Time KYC/KYB

Platforms provide:

- identity verification
- device data
- behavioural signals
- business performance

Banks can skip:

- slow onboarding
- repeated document checks

AI maps:

- identity
- business legitimacy
- network connections

5.3 Intelligence 3 – AI Detects Fraud Across Platform Ecosystems

Fraudsters exploit ecosystems:

- fake merchants
- synthetic consumer accounts
- collusive loans
- platform arbitrage
- duplicate accounts

AI detects:

- multi-account fraud
- shared device fingerprints.
- triangulation fraud
- money flow manipulation

5.4 Intelligence 4 – AI Predicts Customer Intent

These powers:

- personalised offers
- retention
- upsell
- cross-sell

Banks without AI cannot match platform-level intelligence.

6. The Architecture of AI + Embedded Finance

To deliver intelligent embedded finance, banks must build:

1. **Unified API Gateway**
2. **Real-Time Decision Engine**
3. **Feature Store Integration**
4. **Risk and Fraud Orchestration Layer**
5. **Compliance-as-Code**
6. **Virtual Account System**
7. **Settlement and Reconciliation Engine**

Figure 9.3 – AI-Embedded Finance Architecture

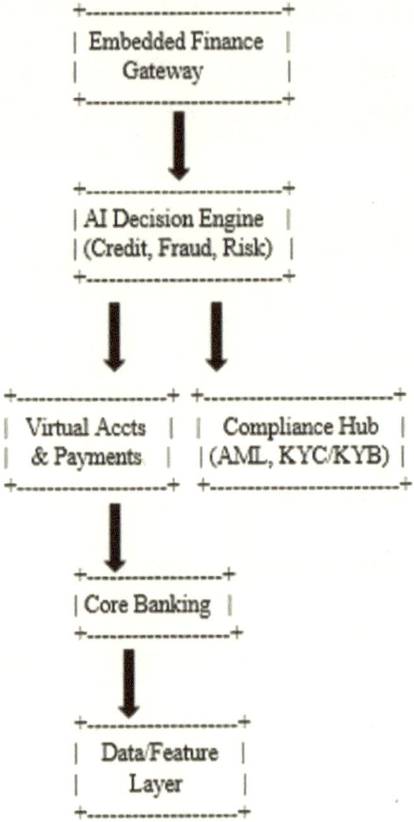

7. How Platforms Become Credit Engines

Platforms see operational signals that banks cannot:

- delivery speed
- worker cancellation rate
- seller dispute frequency
- marketplace visibility
- ratings and reviews

- average order value
- inventory churn

AI converts these signals into:

- risk scores
- cashflow curves
- credit limits
- pricing

Example:

A delivery driver with:

- high acceptance rate
- stable earnings
- few cancellations
- consistent hours
- good ratings

receives:

- higher credit limit
- lower pricing
- instant disbursement

A driver with:

- erratic hours
- high cancellation
- poor ratings

gets:

- lower limits
- lower advance rates

8. Embedded Finance Use Cases Across Industries

8.1 E-Commerce Platforms

- BNPL
- working capital
- inventory finance
- daily sales loans
- seller insurance

8.2 Ride-Hailing and Mobility

- instant payouts
- fuel credit
- vehicle repair loans
- device financing

8.3 Logistics and Supply Chain

- invoice finance
- shipment-based credit
- customs/tax financing
- guarantee and indemnity

8.4 SaaS Platforms

- receivable finance
- subscription-based lending
- partner ecosystem credit

8.5 Social Commerce

- micro-seller loans
- ad-credit finance
- creator payouts

8.6 Travel and Hospitality

- vendor payout finance
- dynamic FX services
- insurance bundles

Embedded finance becomes the **default distribution model**.

9. Why Banks Must Embrace Ecosystem Partnerships

Banks that avoid partnerships face:

1. **Loss of customer relationship**
2. **Loss of distribution**
3. **Loss of relevance**
4. **Loss of data**
5. **Loss of growth**

Banks that embrace partnerships gain:

1. Massive new volumes
2. Better risk models
3. Lower CAC
4. Higher CLV
5. Deeper product penetration

Platforms need:

- regulatory infrastructure
- settlement systems
- liquidity

Banks need:

- customers
- data
- engagement

This creates **mutual dependency**.

10. Business Models: How Banks Monetise Embedded Finance

AI + embedded finance unlocks new revenue streams:

10.1 Revenue Sharing

Banks share:

- fees
- interest
- spreads

with platforms.

10.2 Volume-Based Pricing

Charge:

- per API call
- per transaction

- per payout
- per account

10.3 Data-Driven Lending Margins

Superior intelligence → lower losses → higher margins.

10.4 Subscription Fees

Platforms pay for:

- compliance engines
- risk scoring
- onboarding services

10.5 Cross-Sell Through Ecosystems

- insurance
- FX
- credit
- payroll services

The bank becomes an **intelligence utility**.

11. The Risk Model: AI Makes Embedded Finance Safer

Embedded finance seems risky.

AI makes it less risky than traditional banking because it offers:

1. **More frequent data**
2. **Higher behavioural resolution**
3. **Stronger early-warning signals**

4. **Better segmentation**

5. **Real-time reaction capability**

Figure 9.4 – Why AI Reduces Embedded Finance Risk

TRADITIONAL SME LENDING

- Monthly/annual data
- Static underwriting
- Limited behaviour insights

AI + PLATFORM LENDING

- Daily/hourly data
- Continuous scoring
- Full behaviour visibility
- Network-driven risk

12. Regulatory Evolution: The Future of Platform-Bank Supervision

Regulators now evaluate:

- data flows
- API governance
- shared risk models
- consent management
- outsourced activities
- cross-border flows

AI adds:

- model explainability
- drift management
- fairness
- bias
- data privacy
- algorithmic accountability

Banks must:

- design AI policies
- document model lineage
- audit embedded journeys
- ensure partner KYC/KYB

Embedded finance will become a **co-regulated ecosystem**.

13. The Competitive Moat: Intelligence + Distribution

Banks traditionally won through:

- capital
- regulation
- trust
- distribution

Platforms win through:

- engagement
- data
- intelligence

AI-first banks win through:

- dynamic risk
- real-time decision-making
- personalised pricing
- ecosystem partnerships
- adaptive lending models

The future winner is the one who combines:

- **bank infrastructure**
- **platform engagement**
- **AI intelligence**

Figure 9.5 – The New Competitive Moat

BANKS:	PLATFORMS:	AI-FIRST BANKS:
Capital	Engagement	Capital + Engagement
Compliance	Behaviour Data	Compliance + AI Models
Products	Distribution	Products + Intelligence

14. Case Study Framework: How a Bank Enters a Platform Ecosystem

A bank entering an ecosystem must answer:

1. **Which platform segment?**
    - ride-hailing
    - e-commerce
    - logistics
    - SaaS
2. **What product to embed?**
    - credit
    - payments
    - insurance
    - FX
3. **What data does the platform have?**
    - behavioural
    - operational
    - financial

4. **Where does AI add most value?**
   - underwriting
   - fraud
   - pricing
   - onboarding
5. **What business model works?**
   - revenue share
   - fee-based
   - subscription
6. **What controls must exist?**
   - data governance
   - model oversight
   - risk-sharing agreements

Banks need a **repeatable template.**

15. Platform Banking Maturity Model

Stage 1 – API-Enabled Bank

- basic APIs
- limited partnerships

Stage 2 – Embedded Finance Partnerships

- BNPL
- virtual accounts
- payouts

Stage 3 – AI-Enhanced Embedded Finance

- behaviour-based credit
- real-time risk
- platform-specific offers

Stage 4 – AI Ecosystem Bank

- integrated deeply into multiple ecosystems
- dynamic lending
- shared risk models
- unified intelligence

Figure 9.6 – Platform Banking Maturity Curve

API → EMBEDDED → AI-EMBEDDED → ECOSYSTEM BANK

Conclusion: AI + Platforms + Embedded Finance = The Future of Distribution

Chapter Nine shows how the future of distribution lies in:

- platform ecosystems
- embedded finance
- AI-driven decisioning
- contextual customer journeys
- mutual bank-platform dependency

Banks must evolve from:

controlling distribution → to enabling distribution

owning customers → to powering networks

pushing products → to embedding intelligence

The bank of the future does not sit behind an app.

The bank of the future sits inside **every app**—silently, intelligently, adaptively.

But embedding intelligence across ecosystems is only possible if the bank itself is organised for intelligence, with the right governance, teams, decision systems, and delivery rhythm.

> **"Distribution is no longer where banks sell products. It is where they embed intelligence."**

CHAPTER 10

AI Operating Models for Banks: Rewiring People, Processes, Governance and Culture for Intelligence – First Transformation

"AI is not a technology upgrade; it is an operating-model reinvention."

This chapter provides a deep dive into how operating models must evolve to support intelligence-first banks. It examines organisational design, capability building, AI governance, talent structure, and cross-functional pods. The chapter outlines how AI fundamentally shifts the bank from hierarchical workflows to intelligence-driven networks, where decisions, not departments, become the organising principle.

Behind every AI-first institution is a radical shift in how work gets done. Decisions move from committees to models, processes from manual to autonomous, and organisational structures from rigid hierarchies to fluid intelligence networks. Walk through an AI-native bank, and you'll see pods, agents, decision APIs, and real-time dashboards replacing the old chain of command. The operating model itself becomes a living system.

By this point in the book, we've established that AI transforms:

- decisioning
- products
- credit
- risk
- SME banking
- customer experience
- compliance
- distribution

- platforms
- embedded finance

But **none of these transformations can scale**, if the organisation still operates like:

- a digital bank
- or worse, a legacy bank

AI is not software you implement.

AI is a **new institutional architecture**.

It changes:

- how teams work
- how decisions are made
- how departments coordinate
- how products evolve
- how risk is managed
- how culture flows
- how governance operates
- how talent is hired
- how budgets are allocated

This chapter explains the **AI Operating Model** – the blueprint for how an intelligent bank functions internally.

We'll cover:

1. Operating-model transformation
2. AI-first organisational structure
3. Decision architectures
4. Data governance
5. Product and engineering alignment

6. Risk, model governance, and oversight
7. AI factories, pods, and squads
8. Talent, culture, and skills
9. Budgeting and investment
10. Execution roadmaps

By the end, you will have a complete transformation blueprint for building an AI-first institution.

1. Why the Traditional Operating Model Fails in the AI Era

Legacy banks operate like:

- bureaucracies
- with rigid hierarchies
- siloed teams
- periodic decision cycles
- slow approvals
- committee-driven governance
- project-based delivery

Digital transformation improved:

- automation
- channels
- journeys
- cloud adoption

But it did not change:

- organisational structure
- human workflows

- governance cadence
- decision opacity

AI-first banking requires:

- continuous change
- rapid experimentation
- real-time decisions
- collaborative pods
- model oversight
- cross-functional delivery

1.1 Five Structural Weaknesses of Traditional Operating Models

1. **Silos block intelligence**

   Risk doesn't talk to product.

   Product doesn't talk to fraud.

   Fraud doesn't talk to compliance.

   Data sits everywhere and nowhere.

2. **Decision cycles are slow**

   Committees meet weekly or monthly.

   AI needs decisions in milliseconds.

3. **Projects, not platforms**

   Banks run projects, not long-term platforms.

4. **IT seen as support, not a strategy**

   AI needs engineering at the centre.

5. **Risk frameworks built for rules, not models**

   Traditional risk governance collapses in model-driven environments.

1.2 The Result?

- AI stuck in pilots
- High false positives
- Slow approvals
- Compliance concerns
- Model drift
- Organisational resistance
- Multiple "AI teams" but no real intelligence

2. The AI-First Operating Model: A New Institutional Blueprint

An AI-first bank must operate like:

- a technology company
- a data science institution
- a risk intelligence hub
- a behavioural analytics firm

The AI-first operating model has **four pillars**:

1. **AI Strategy and Governance**
2. **AI Delivery and Architecture**
3. **AI Talent and Culture**
4. **AI Business Alignment and Value Realisation**

Figure 10.1 – The Four Pillars of the AI Operating Model

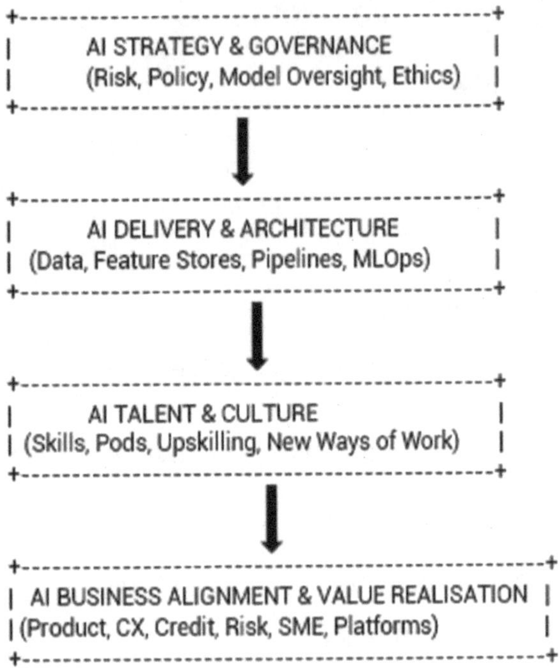

3. AI Strategy and Governance: The Institutional Anchors

AI cannot scale without:

- policies
- governance committees
- model oversight
- ethical guidelines
- regulatory alignment

3.1 Governance Structure

The AI-first bank requires:

(1) AI Strategy Office (AISO)

- sets AI direction
- aligns business, product, risk, tech

(2) Model Governance Committee (MGC)

- approves models
- oversees retraining
- manages drift
- ensures fairness and explainability

(3) Data Governance Council (DGC)

- stewards data quality, privacy, lineage

(4) Ethics and Responsible AI Board (RAI)

- review bias
- fairness
- impact assessments

(5) AI Risk Office (AIRO)

- evaluates model risk
- calibrates thresholds
- oversees operational risk of AI

Figure 10.2 – AI Governance Structure

```
BOARD
|
|--> Responsible AI Board
        |
        +--> AI Strategy Office (AISO)
        |
        +--> Model Governance Committee (MGC)
        |
        +--> Data Governance Council (DGC)
        |
        +--> AI Risk Office (AIRO)
```

4. AI Delivery and Architecture: The Engine Room

Digital transformation required:

- DevOps
- APIs
- cloud
- microservices

AI transformation requires:

- MLOps
- feature stores
- vector databases
- real-time stream processing
- online/offline training
- experimentation pipelines

4.1 Core Components of AI Delivery

1. **Data Lake and Real-Time Pipelines**
2. **Feature Store**
3. **Model Training Infrastructure**
4. **Experimentation Platform**
5. **Online Model Serving**
6. **Monitoring, Drift and Alerting**
7. **Feedback Loops**
8. **Human Override Management**

4.2 The AI Factory

The AI factory is a:

- permanent
- continuously running
- iterative
- cross-functional

system that produces:

- models
- features
- experiments
- updates
- improvements

Figure 10.3 – The AI Factory

DATA ----> FEATURES ----> MODELS ----> DEPLOY ----> MONITOR ----> FEEDBACK ----> (back to data)

5. AI Talent and Org Structure: Pods, Squads and Fusion Teams

Traditional banks use:

- departments
- hierarchies
- approval chains

AI-first banks use:

- cross-functional pods
- full-stack teams

- product-led orgs
- engineering-first mindset

5.1 The AI Product Pod

A pod consists of:

- 1 Product Owner
- 2–3 Data Scientists
- 2–3 ML Engineers
- 1–2 Backend Engineers
- 1 Risk Analyst
- 1 UX/Behavioural Designer
- 1 Compliance Liaison

Pods own:

- risk models
- pricing engine
- fraud engine
- credit engine
- onboarding journey

Product outcomes, not departments, unify pods.

Figure 10.4 – AI Product Pod Structure

```
PRODUCT OWNER
|
+-- Data Science
|        |- DS1
|        |- DS2
|
+-- ML Engineering
|        |- MLE1
|        |- MLE2
|
+-- Backend Engineering
|        |- BE1
|        |- BE2
|
+-- Risk Analyst
|
+-- Compliance Liaison
|
+-- UX / Behaviour Designer
```

6. Organisational Structure of an AI-First Bank

The new bank org structure is a **mesh**, not a hierarchy.

Three layers drive everything:

1. **Decision Layer (Models and Intelligence)**
2. **Product Layer (Pods and Squads)**
3. **Platform Layer (Engineering and Data)**

Gone are:

- product silos
- channel silos
- risk siloing
- compliance dead-ends

AI forces **integration**.

6.1 The AI Mesh Organisation

Figure 10.5 – The AI Mesh Organisation

```
          +------------------+
          | DECISION LAYER |
          | (Model Engines)  |
          +---------+--------+
                    |
          +--------------------+--------------------+
          |                    |
+-----------+                  +----------------+
| PRODUCT  |                   | PRODUCT        |
| POD A    |                   | POD B          |
+-----------+                  +----------------+
          |                    |
          +--------------------+--------------------+
                    |
          +--------------------+
          | PLATFORM LAYER |
          |    (Data + Engg)   |
          +--------------------+
```

7. Decision Architecture: The New 'Core Banking'

Chapter One established that:

Decisioning is the new core banking.

This means:

- the decision engine becomes the most critical internal system
- risk, fraud, credit, pricing, onboarding, collections all converge
- models replace hard-coded rules

7.1 The Decision Engine Must Be

- real-time
- scalable

- explainable
- traceable
- adaptive
- compliant
- observable

7.2 Decision Architecture Layers

1. Request Orchestration
2. Feature Retrieval
3. Model Execution
4. Risk/Compliance Overrides
5. Decision Output
6. Logging and Explainability

Figure 10.6 – The Decision Engine Pipeline

Request --> Feature Lookup --> Model Scoring --> Policy/Compliance Layer --> Decision --> Log + Explain

8. Data Governance: The Nervous System of AI

AI-first banks must upgrade:

1. **Data Ownership**

   Clear owners for:

   - quality
   - lineage
   - timeliness

2. **Data Contracts**

   Guarantees about:

- structure
- schema
- freshness

3. **Data Catalogues**

   Universal metadata system

4. **Privacy and Consent**

   Customer must know:

   - what data is used
   - for what purpose

5. **Data Quality SLAs**

   If the data breaks, the model breaks.

6. **Data Stewardship Roles**

   Dedicated experts maintain data health.

9. Product and Engineering Operating Rhythm

AI-first banks integrate product and engineering through:

Weekly:

- model performance reviews
- drift analysis
- experiment updates

Bi-Weekly:

- feature pipeline planning
- product roadmap alignment

Monthly:

- cross-functional risk and compliance calibration

- business value tracking
- customer behaviour insights

Quarterly:

- model retraining plans
- architecture review
- AI strategy refresh

This creates a predictable cycle for continuous improvement.

10. Risk, Compliance and AI Governance

AI introduces:

- model risk
- explainability risk
- fairness risk
- privacy risk
- regulatory risk

Traditional compliance teams are not equipped for this.

10.1 New Roles Needed

- Model Risk Analysts
- Explainability Engineers
- AI Auditors
- Responsible AI Officers
- Behavioural Risk Analysts
- Data Ethics Specialists

10.2 Model Risk Lifecycle

The lifecycle includes:

1. Design
2. Training
3. Testing
4. Approval
5. Deployment
6. Monitoring
7. Retraining
8. Decommissioning

Figure 10.7 – Model Risk Lifecycle

DESIGN --> TRAIN --> TEST --> APPROVE --> DEPLOY --> MONITOR --> RETRAIN --> RETIRE

11. AI Factories, Labs and Experimentation Culture

Experimentation becomes a core part of the bank.

11.1 AI Factory

Runs continuous improvement on:

- feature sets
- risk models
- fraud models
- pricing engines

11.2 AI Lab

Works on:

- future concepts
- LLM use cases
- conversational banking
- identity biometrics
- behavioural analytics

11.3 Experimentation Culture

Accepts:

- small failures
- rapid testing
- scientific mindset

Banks must shift from:

"What is the ROI before we begin?"

to

"What is the cost of not experimenting?"

12. Skills and Talent: The Workforce of an AI-First Bank

The AI-first bank needs three categories of talent:

12.1 Category 1: Builders

- ML Engineers
- Data Scientists
- Data Engineers
- Software Engineers
- Platform Engineers
- MLOps Engineers

These people build intelligence.

12.2 Category 2: Translators

- Product Owners
- Business Analysts
- Risk Modellers
- compliance technologists
- Customer Journey Designers

Translators connect the business with the AI factory.

12.3 Category 3: Governors

- Responsible AI Leaders
- Model Risk Officers
- AI Auditors
- Compliance and Ethics Leaders

Governors ensure AI is safe, stable, fair and compliant.

13. Cultural Transformation: From Risk-Avoiding to Experiment-Driven

Legacy culture:

- avoid mistakes
- follow rules
- escalate issues
- move slowly

AI culture:

- run experiments
- learn from data
- challenge assumptions

- fail small, succeed big
- trust teams
- democratise knowledge

13.1 What Must Change?

1. **Speed > Perfection**
2. **Feedback > Hierarchy**
3. **Decentralisation > Control**
4. **Learning > Compliance-Only**
5. **Transparency > Secrecy**

13.2 The AI-Mindset Bank

The AI-first bank embraces:

- curiosity
- iteration
- automation
- intelligence.
- collaboration.

14. Budgeting and Investment: Funding an AI-First Bank

AI transformation requires investment in:

1. **Data foundation**
2. **Feature store**
3. **Pipelines**
4. **Model infrastructure**
5. **Cloud architecture**

6. **Pods and cross-functional teams**
7. **Responsible AI governance**
8. **Platforms and APIs**
9. **Talent acquisition**
10. **Experiment labs**

14.1 New Funding Model: Platform Funding

Banks must shift from:

- project budgets → to platform budgets
- capex-heavy → to opex-flexible
- once-and-done → to continuous funding

15. AI Execution Roadmap: How to Build an AI-First Bank

A bank becomes AI-first in **four phases**:

Phase 1 – Foundations

- data lake
- pipelines
- feature store
- initial models (risk, identity)
- governance

Phase 2 – Expansion

- full decision engine
- dynamic risk
- fraud intelligence
- behavioural credit
- adaptive pricing

Phase 3 – Distribution

- embedded finance
- SME platforms
- ecosystem integrations

Phase 4 – Intelligence Everywhere

- autonomous journeys
- AI copilots
- predictive customer insights
- real-time RM engines
- AI governance at scale

Figure 10.8 – AI Execution Roadmap

FOUNDATIONS → EXPANSION → DISTRIBUTION → INTELLIGENCE AT SCALE

Conclusion: The AI Operating Model Is the True Transformation

This chapter established that building an AI-first bank requires:

- new governance
- new org structures
- new decision engines
- new talent
- new data systems
- new cultural principles
- new product delivery rhythms
- new risk models

- new budgets
- new execution roadmaps

Technology alone cannot make a bank intelligent.

Only an intelligent operating model can.

In Chapter Eleven, we move from how banks build intelligence internally to how regulators must supervise it externally, because when decisions become models, supervision must become model-aware, continuous, and audit-ready.

"AI doesn't fit into the old operating model. It demands a new one—one that thinks, evolves, and rewires itself."

CHAPTER 11

AI-First Regulation and Supervisory Frameworks: How Regulators Must Evolve for the Age of Intelligent Banking

"Regulators must learn to supervise algorithms, not just institutions."

This chapter rethinks regulation for an intelligence-led financial system, arguing that traditional frameworks anchored in periodic reporting and rule-based supervision cannot keep up with algorithmic institutions. It explores how supervisors must evolve to oversee models, data pipelines, agents, and autonomous decision systems. The chapter positions regulators as the architects of safe, transparent, and accountable AI adoption.

Regulators were built to supervise documents, reports, and periodic filings, yet they now face institutions that execute millions of model-driven decisions per minute. Supervising algorithms requires new supervisory artefacts: model inventories, drift dashboards, explainability logs, bias tests, and real-time risk telemetry. The future regulator supervises models, not paperwork.

"Regulation lagged behind digital transformation, but it cannot lag behind AI."

"The regulator of an AI-first bank must itself become an AI-first regulator."

Banks have entered the AI era faster than regulators have.

But AI touches every dimension that regulators care about:

- risk
- fairness
- consumer protection
- AML
- market stability

- privacy
- ethics
- explainability
- governance

AI is not a feature; AI rewires the entire banking system.

Regulators know this.

But their supervisory frameworks were built for:

- rules
- human decisions
- documents
- checklists
- periods (monthly/quarterly)
- static models
- linear processes

AI operates:

- continuously
- behaviourally
- adaptively
- dynamically
- probabilistically
- through feedback loops
- with models that learn over time

This mismatch creates a **regulatory gap**.

Chapter Eleven explains:

1. Why AI demands new supervisory thinking
1. The risks regulators must oversee
2. The AI supervisory architecture
3. Model governance frameworks
4. Data governance and privacy standards
5. Explainability and transparency expectations
6. AML and fraud oversight in the AI era
7. Cross-border supervision for AI-first banks
8. The regulator's own use of AI
9. Global regulatory trends shaping intelligent finance

By the end, you will see that **the future of regulation is intelligence-based, not compliance-based**.

1. The Regulatory Gap: AI Moves Faster Than Policy

Digital transformation took banks 10–15 years.

AI transformation took 18–36 months.

Regulators were prepared for:

- digital KYC
- cloud frameworks
- cyber risk
- outsourcing guidelines
- API governance
- consumer protection in digital channels

But AI introduces:

- dynamic credit limits
- algorithmic pricing
- behaviour-based risk
- adaptive fraud detection
- graph-based AML intelligence
- continuous identity
- models that evolve

Traditional regulation cannot handle this.

1.1 The Three Regulatory Gaps

Gap 1 – Speed

Regulation moves yearly.

AI moves hourly.

Gap 2 – Transparency

AI models are complex.

Regulators need visibility into black boxes.

Gap 3 – Explainability

AI decisions must be explainable to:

- customers
- auditors
- courts
- regulators

This is the new frontier.

2. The AI Risk Landscape: What Regulators Must Protect Against

AI introduces seven new categories of risk.

2.1 Risk 1 – Model Risk

Models may:

- drift
- degrade
- become biased
- become unstable
- lose accuracy
- misinterpret signals

Regulators must track:

- data quality
- model inputs
- performance metrics
- retraining cycles
- overrides

2.2 Risk 2 – Bias and Fairness

AI can unintentionally:

- discriminate by geography
- create correlated biases
- penalise certain behaviours
- reflect biased historical data

Fairness frameworks become mandatory.

2.3 Risk 3 – Explainability Risk

Customers must understand:

- why they were rejected
- why limits changed
- why fraud was flagged
- why pricing fluctuated

Explainability is a consumer right.

2.4 Risk 4 – Data Privacy Risk

AI requires:

- behavioural data
- network data
- device intelligence
- transaction patterns

Regulators must ensure:

- consent
- ethical use
- minimisation
- purpose limitation

2.5 Risk 5 – Algorithmic Collusion

In markets with many AI-driven institutions:

- pricing models can converge
- risk models can react similarly
- collective outcomes may emerge

This poses competition risks.

2.6 Risk 6 – Concentration Risk

If multiple banks use:

- the same AI vendor
- the same APIs
- the same cloud
- the same foundation model

Systemic risk increases.

2.7 Risk 7 – Black Box Risk

Some models are:

- too complex
- too opaque
- too autonomous

Regulators must demand transparency.

3. The AI Supervisory Model: A New Regulatory Architecture

Regulators must shift from:

- periodic audits
- rule-based supervision
- document-based reviews

to:

- continuous supervision
- model-based reviews
- data-driven oversight

3.1 New Supervisory Pillars

1. **Model Governance Supervision**
2. **AI Risk Management Supervision**
3. **Data Governance Supervision**
4. **Algorithmic Fairness Supervision**
5. **Consumer Protection in AI Decisions**
6. **AI/ML Documentation and Explainability**
7. **Operational and Concentration Risk**
8. **Third-Party AI Vendor Management**

Figure 11.1 – The AI Supervisory Architecture

```
+-------------------------------------------------+
| MODEL GOVERNANCE & RISK OVERSIGHT               |
+-------------------------------------------------+
| DATA GOVERNANCE & PRIVACY                       |
+-------------------------------------------------+
| ALGORITHM FAIRNESS & ETHICS                     |
+-------------------------------------------------+
| AI CONSUMER PROTECTION & DISCLOSURES            |
+-------------------------------------------------+
| THIRD-PARTY & CLOUD AI CONCENTRATION RISK |
+-------------------------------------------------+
```

4. Model Governance: The Heart of AI Regulation

Regulators must evaluate:

- training data
- feature sets
- validation tests
- sensitivity analysis
- bias audits

- hyperparameter tuning
- model drift detection
- override ratios
- performance metrics

4.1 The Model Governance Framework

Regulators will require banks to adopt:

1. **Model Inventory Register**
2. **Model Risk Classification System**
3. **Model Lifecycle Documentation**
4. **Performance Monitoring SLAs**
5. **Bias-Testing Protocols**
6. **Explainability Controls**
7. **Fallback and Override Procedures**
8. **Retraining Logs**

Figure 11.2 – Model Lifecycle Oversight

Train --> Validate --> Approve --> Deploy --> Monitor --> Retrain --> Revalidate --> Retire

5. Data Governance in the AI Era

AI requires:

- more data
- more sensitive data
- more continuous data
- more behavioural data

Regulators must enforce:

5.1 Data Quality Standards

Poor data = dangerous models

5.2 Data Lineage

Every data point must be traceable to its source.

5.3 Data Consent Frameworks

Customers must opt-in for sensitive data use.

5.4 Data Minimisation

Use only what is necessary.

5.5 Data Localisation

Some jurisdictions require:

- local storage
- local processing

5.6 Data Sharing Protocols

APIs must be secure and monitored.

6. Explainability: The New Consumer Protection Frontier

AI decisions must be explainable to:

- customers
- internal teams
- regulators

Explainability must be:

Human-readable

Simple language.

No model math.

Actionable

Gives customers a path to improve.

Consistent

Same explanation for similar cases.

Auditable

Logs stored for regulatory review.

Figure 11.3 – Components of Explainability

```
+----------------------------+
| Model Insight Summary      |
+----------------------------+
| Key Features Influencing   |
| Decision                   |
+----------------------------+
| Clear Human Explanation    |
+--------------------------- +
| Customer Improvement Path  |
+----------------------------+
| Regulator Audit Log        |
+----------------------------+
```

7. Fairness and Bias: Regulation for Ethical AI

AI can unintentionally:

- disadvantage minorities
- penalise certain behaviours
- amplify past bias
- correlate features with sensitive attributes

Regulators will enforce:

7.1 Fairness Metrics

- disparate impact
- equal opportunity
- predictive parity

7.2 Feature Sensitivity Audits

Features cannot proxy sensitive attributes.

7.3 Bias Mitigation Procedures

Banks must show:

- reweighting
- balancing
- data balancing

Banks must prove fairness.

8. AML and Fraud Regulation in the AI Age

AI transforms AML from:

- periodic monitoring
- sample-based analysis
- rules-based systems

to:

continuous surveillance

graph-based intelligence

anomaly detection

network clustering

Regulators will require:

8.1 Network-Based AML Models

8.2 Entity-Linking and Beneficial Ownership AI

8.3 Continuous Transaction Monitoring

8.4 Alert Explainability

8.5 Reduced False Positives

(see Figure 11.4)

Figure 11.4 – AI AML Graph Supervision

```
Customer A -----> Merchant X -----> Customer B
   |              |
   |              -----> Supplier Y
   |
   -----> Device Z -----> Customer C
```

AI flags:

- Linkages
- Suspicious flows
- Network risk

9. Cross-Border AI Regulation: Global Co-Supervision

AI introduces cross-border challenges:

9.1 Data Flows

Models may use:

- cloud
- cross-country data

9.2 Global Model Drift

Economic shocks in one region propagate elsewhere.

9.3 Multi-Jurisdiction Fairness Rules

Different markets have:

different protected attributes

different bias rules

9.4 Cross-Border Platforms

Bigtech and fintech operate globally.

Regulators must collaborate across borders.

10. The Regulator's Own Use of AI

Regulators must become **AI-powered supervisors**.

AI for regulators includes:

10.1 Supervisory AI

Model monitoring tools.

Dynamic dashboards.

Real-time risk scores.

10.2 Surveillance AI

Detect systemic anomalies.

10.3 Conduct Supervision AI

Detect misconduct using:

- behavioural patterns
- communications analysis

10.4 Macroprudential AI

Predict financial system stress.

Regulators must upgrade themselves.

Figure 11.5 – AI for Regulators

```
DATA STREAMS --> RISK AI --> SUPERVISORY ACTIONS
            |
            +--> Conduct AI
            |
            +--> Macroprudential AI
```

11. Third-Party and AI Vendor Regulation

Banks often use:

- cloud providers
- AI vendors
- API providers
- model marketplaces
- Regtech and Fintech partners

Regulators will enforce:

11.1 Vendor Certification

11.2 Model Transparency

11.3 Data Access Limitations

11.4 Resilience and SLAs

11.5 Exit and Migration Plans

12. Ethical AI: The Moral Dimension of Banking

Ethical requirements include:

12.1 Human Oversight

AI cannot make irreversible decisions alone.

12.2 Accountability

Banks remain responsible for model outcomes.

12.3 Redress Mechanisms

Customers must appeal decisions.

12.4 Transparency in Data Usage

Clear communication.

12.5 No Manipulative Personalisation

No exploiting behavioural vulnerabilities.

13. The Regulatory Maturity Curve

Regulators evolve in four phases:

Phase 1 – Digital Regulator

Rules updated for:

- online banking
- digital KYC

Phase 2 – Data Regulator

Focus on:

- privacy
- consent
- data protection laws

Phase 3 – AI-Aware Regulator

Creates:

- model oversight
- fairness frameworks

Phase 4 – AI-First Regulator

Operates:

- real-time supervision
- AI-enabled monitoring

Figure 11.6 – Regulatory Maturity Curve

DIGITAL → DATA → AI-AWARE → AI-FIRST

Conclusion: The Regulator of the Future Must Become an Intelligent Institution

AI-first banking requires:

- AI-first supervision

- AI-first oversight
- AI-first fairness frameworks
- AI-first AML
- AI-first consumer protection

Regulation must evolve from:

- periodic reporting → continuous insight
- human rules → algorithmic oversight
- document audits → model governance
- local frameworks → cross-border collaboration
- reactive → anticipatory

The regulator becomes:

- a data steward
- an AI overseer
- a fairness guardian
- a systemic risk oracle

AI does not reduce the role of regulation.

AI **magnifies** it.

In Chapter Twelve, we move from supervision to execution—how LLMs and agentic systems reshape underwriting, service, operations, and knowledge work, and why "cognitive automation" becomes the next operating layer of the bank.

"Regulators don't restrain AI—they refine it, so intelligence can scale safely across society."

CHAPTER 12

LLMs, Agents and Autonomous Workflows

"Generative AI does not automate tasks. It automates thinking."

This chapter demystifies how LLMs, agents, and autonomous workflows will transform internal operations across the bank. It explains how banks can deploy swarms of intelligent agents for underwriting, compliance, operations, treasury, and customer service. It highlights why generative AI is not just a tool for efficiency but a cognitive engine that can analyse, reason, decide, and act in real time.

Inside tomorrow's bank, thousands of intelligent agents will work side by side with humans scanning patterns, drafting reports, resolving disputes, validating transactions, and steering decisions. These agents don't sleep, don't forget, and don't wait for instructions. They proactively act on signals from data, design workflows on the fly, and orchestrate processes end-to-end. Banks evolve from manual operations to autonomous ones.

"LLMs aren't here to automate tasks. They are here to automate thinking."

"LLMs turn language into infrastructure and infrastructure into action."

"Agents don't just assist the bank. They change what the bank is capable of becoming."

If Chapters 1–11 explained the **intelligence of the bank**, this chapter explains the **intelligence of the workforce**—how LLMs, GPT-class agents, and autonomous decisioning systems transform banking operations at a cognitive level.

For decades, banks tried to automate:

- forms
- approvals
- workflows
- signatures

- tickets
- escalations

But the one thing they could never automate was **thinking**—the unstructured interpretation and judgement that humans do:

- reading documents
- understanding context
- interpreting regulations
- making sense of conversations
- writing notes
- summarising risks
- advising customers
- analysing market data

LLMs change this.

This chapter explains how banks deploy LLMs to transform:

1. Customer service and conversational banking
2. Operations
3. Documentation and compliance
4. Underwriting
5. Credit memos
6. Internal knowledge management
7. Product teams
8. Software engineering
9. Analyst workflows
10. Assistants, agents and autonomous decision systems

And how banks build a **Responsible LLM Architecture** that is compliant, safe, and explainable.

1. Why LLMs Are Different From Previous Automation Tools

Banks have used automation for decades:

- RPA (Robotic Process Automation)
- BPM (Business Process Management)
- workflows
- scripts
- macros
- templates
- bots

These tools automate **actions**, not **intelligence**.

RPA cannot:

- understand unstructured content
- infer meaning
- write natural language
- converse
- contextualise
- problem-solve
- interpret ambiguity

LLMs do all of this.

1.1 LLMs Are Cognitive Engines

LLMs are trained on trillions of words and can:

- interpret
- summarise
- classify
- extract

- translate
- generate
- reason
- explain

This is not automation.

This is **cognitive augmentation**.

1.2 The Bank of the Future Uses Three Intelligence Layers

1. **Decision Models** – mathematical, numerical, structured
2. **Language Models (LLMs)** – unstructured intelligence
3. **Agents** – autonomous systems that take action

Figure 12.1 – The Three Intelligence Layers

```
+----------------------------+
| DECISION MODELS (AI)       |
| • Fraud                    |
| • Credit                   |
| • Pricing                  |
+-------------+--------------+
              ↓
+------------------------------+
| LANGUAGE MODELS (LLMs)       |
| • Reasoning                  |
| • Understanding              |
| • Natural language           |
+-------------+----------------+
              ↓
+------------------------------+
| AGENTS (AUTONOMOUS)          |
| • Take actions               |
| • Execute workflows          |
| • Multi-step reasoning       |
+------------------------------+
```

2. Conversational Banking: The New Front Door of the Bank

Conversation is the new interface.

The app is no longer the product—the conversation is.

LLMs enable:

- natural language onboarding
- contextual financial advice
- conversational dispute resolution
- real-time fraud explanations
- personalised insights
- predictive nudges
- dynamic FAQs

2.1 Conversation Replaces Navigation

In traditional apps, customers must:

- click
- search
- scroll
- guess

With LLMs, customers simply:

"I need to increase my limit for a flight booking."

"Explain why my payment was blocked."

"Show me my expenses for the last 3 months."

"Predict my cashflow for next week."

"Tell me if I can afford this purchase."

LLMs understand intent, not clicks.

(see Figure 12.2)

Figure 12.2 – How LLM Frontends Replace App Navigation

WITHOUT LLM:

Menu → Cards → Limits → Edit → Submit

WITH LLM:

"Increase my limit to $2,000 for the next 24 hours."

3. AI in Operations: The Cognitive Back Office

Operations teams are the hidden engine of banking:

- verifications
- document checks
- reconciliations
- escalations
- customer emails
- dispute management
- case notes
- exception handling

These tasks involve **language**, **interpretation**, **review**, and **decision support**—perfect territory for LLMs.

3.1 LLMs Reduce Operational Load by 40–70%

LLMs can:

- summarise case files
- draft responses
- analyse disputes

- extract fields from documents
- classify issues
- suggest next actions
- highlight risks
- create structured reports

3.2 Example: Dispute Operations

Traditional workflow:

- agent reads long complaint
- checks transactions
- reviews ledger
- writes response
- logs notes

LLM workflow:

- LLM reads everything
- extracts the issue
- drafts the response
- suggests resolution
- writes internal log

Agent simply confirms.

4. Documentation and Compliance: LLMs Are Built for This

Banking is:

- forms
- contracts

- policies
- procedures
- circulars
- regulatory notices
- compliance manuals

LLMs transform this universe.

4.1 Regulatory Interpretation

LLMs can:

- interpret regulatory text
- summarise mandates
- map requirements to internal processes
- highlight non-compliant areas
- generate audit checklists

4.2 Policy Generation

LLMs draft:

- AML policies
- KYC procedures
- data governance documents
- risk frameworks
- operational guidelines

4.3 Document Intelligence

LLMs extract data from:

- PDFs

- scanned documents
- contracts
- invoices
- statements

(see Figure 12.3)

Figure 12.3 – LLM Compliance Workflow

Regulation --> LLM Interpreter --> Risk Mapping --> Gap Analysis --> Action Plan

5. Underwriting: The Human + LLM Superpowers

Underwriting involves:

- reading financials
- interpreting ratios
- evaluating patterns
- assessing compliance
- summarising risk

LLMs augment this dramatically.

5.1 LLMs Produce

- financial summaries
- risk notes
- red flags
- exceptions
- sector analysis
- qualitative commentary

5.2 Humans Still Do:

- judgement
- ethical evaluation
- contextual interpretation
- final decision

LLMs give underwriters **superhuman comprehension speed**.

6. Credit Memos: 80% Automated by LLMs

A credit memo contains:

- financial summary
- risk assessment
- business overview
- exposure analysis
- cashflow analysis
- recommendation

LLMs can generate:

- entire memos
- risk sections
- industry outlook
- behavioural analysis

This frees underwriters to focus on **judgement, not typing**.

7. Knowledge Management: LLMs Turn Banks Into Neural Networks

Banks produce enormous knowledge:

- internal policies

- product manuals
- training docs
- compliance rules
- process maps

But these are:

- scattered
- outdated
- hard to navigate

LLMs convert all this into an **intelligent knowledge engine**.

7.1 Employees Can Ask

- "What is the KYC requirement for SMEs?"
- "How do we process insurance claims?"
- "What is the FX policy for corporate clients?"
- "What are the acceptable risk parameters?"

LLMs search, summarise, and answer instantly.

(see Figure 12.4)

Figure 12.4 – The Bank-as-a-Knowledge-Network

Policies + Manuals + Product Docs + SOPs

↓

LLM Knowledge Layer

↓

Employees ask questions in natural language

8. Product Teams: LLMs Speed Up Discovery, Definition and Deployment

Product teams rely on:

- user research
- discovery
- backlog creation
- requirements drafting
- competitor analysis
- customer interviews
- analytics

LLMs accelerate all of this.

8.1 Discovery

LLMs analyse:

- surveys
- complaints
- transcripts
- behavioural logs

8.2 Definition

LLMs create:

- PRDs
- user stories
- acceptance criteria

8.3 Deployment

LLMs create:

- release notes
- communication drafts

Product cycles shrink from **12 weeks to 3–5 weeks**.

9. Engineering: LLMs as Developer Copilots

Software development is transformed by:

- GPT-based coding copilots
- code generation
- debugging assistance
- test case writing
- documentation automation

9.1 LLMs Speed Up

- writing code
- understanding legacy systems
- generating microservices
- fixing vulnerabilities
- explaining code behaviour

9.2 The Bank's Dev Productivity Jumps 30–50%

LLMs turn every engineer into a:

- faster coder
- better debugger
- more accurate tester

10. Analyst Workflows: AI Becomes the Analyst

Analysts do:

- research
- data analysis
- insight generation

- report writing
- financial modelling
- competitive intelligence

LLMs transform this.

10.1 LLMs Do the Busy Work

- summarising industry news
- extracting useful insights
- generating decks
- writing reports

10.2 Analysts Do the Thinking Work

- strategy
- interpretation
- explanation
- recommendations

11. Agents: Autonomous Workflows Become Reality

LLMs can **think**, but agents can **act**.

AI agents can:

- perform tasks
- trigger workflows
- retrieve data
- call APIs
- run multi-step automations

- escalate cases
- generate reports

11.1 Example: Credit Agent

The agent:

- retrieves customer data
- checks cashflow
- updates features
- runs model prediction
- drafts credit memo
- sends for approval

11.2 Example: Fraud Agent

The agent:

- reads suspicious transaction
- runs graph analysis
- compares against typologies
- drafts alert outcome
- suggests escalation

12. Multi-Agent Systems: The Future Bank-as-an-AI-Org

Banks will eventually operate multi-agent ecosystems:

- onboarding agent
- risk agent
- fraud agent
- AML agent

- pricing agent
- collections agent
- customer experience agent
- SME advisory agent

These agents communicate and coordinate.

(see Figure 12.5)

Figure 12.5 – Multi-Agent Bank System

```
ONBOARDING AGENT <--> RISK AGENT <--> FRAUD AGENT
   |                     |
   |                     |
CX AGENT <----------> PRICING AGENT <--------+
   |
SME ADVISORY AGENT
```

13. Responsible LLM Architecture: The Bank's New Compliance Requirement

Banks cannot use LLMs recklessly.

They require architecture-level controls.

13.1 Core Components

1. **Guardrails**
2. **Prompt Monitoring**
3. **Redaction / Masking**
4. **Policy Enforcement Layer**
5. **Safety Classifiers**
6. **Data Privacy Filters**
7. **Role-Based Access**

8. **Audit Logs**
9. **Explainability Tools**

(see Figure 12.6)

Figure 12.6 – Responsible LLM Stack

USER PROMPT

↓

GUARDRAIL LAYER

↓

LLM ENGINE

↓

SAFETY FILTERS + AUDIT LOGS

↓

OUTPUT

14. AI + LLM Governance: A New Oversight Framework

Regulators require:

- transparency
- explainability
- privacy protection
- ethical boundaries
- human supervision

Banks must create:

1. **LLM Risk Committee**
2. **Safety Evaluation Framework**

3. **Red Teaming Protocols**
4. **Misuse Prevention Procedures**
5. **Hallucination Risk Controls**

15. Talent Transformation: Every Employee Becomes AI-Augmented

LLMs empower:

- analysts
- underwriters
- risk officers
- compliance staff
- RMs
- call centre agents
- credit teams
- product designers
- data analysts
- software engineers

The new bank workforce is:

- faster
- more accurate
- more informed
- more consistent
- more scalable

15.1 Mandatory AI Literacy

Training required in:

- prompting
- oversight
- red flags

- AI ethics
- model interpretation

Through this transformation, every employee becomes an **AI operator**.

16. The Bank-as-an-AI-Organism

When LLMs, decision models, and agents are integrated, the bank becomes:

- self-learning
- self-correcting
- self-improving
- self-optimising

This is the shift from:

- manual workflows → autonomous workflows
- human interpretation → AI interpretation
- rule-based execution → intelligence-based execution

The bank begins to behave like a **living organism**.

(see Figure 12.7)

Figure 12.7 – The AI-Organism Bank

SENSE (LLMs + Signals)

↓

THINK (Models + Agents)

↓

ACT (Decision Engine + Workflows)

↓

LEARN (Feedback + Retraining)

Conclusion: LLMs Are the Mind of the AI-First Bank

Decision models power the institution.

But LLMs power the **thinking** of the institution.

LLMs:

- enhance every workflow
- accelerate every team
- increase accuracy
- improve compliance
- reduce errors
- improve underwriting
- transform customer service
- strengthen risk and fraud detection
- democratise knowledge
- automate reasoning
- enable autonomous agents

Chapter Twelve demonstrates:

- how LLMs rewire banks
- how agents automate complex work
- how the workforce becomes AI-augmented
- how cognitive automation replaces manual interpretation

In Chapter Thirteen, we zoom out from workflows to the endgame: what banking becomes by 2030 when intelligence is the interface, decisions are continuous, and agents run operations at scale.

"The future workforce isn't man or machine—it's the harmony between the two."

CHAPTER 13

The AI-First Bank of 2030

"The bank of 2030 is not a place you go. It is intelligence that follows you."

Peering into the near future, this chapter paints a detailed picture of what a fully AI-driven bank will look like by 2030. It explores autonomous branches, invisible onboarding, real-time credit, hyper-personalised financial advice, intelligent fraud networks, and agent-driven operations. The chapter offers a vivid, evidence-backed vision of the bank that follows the customer everywhere—not the other way around.

Picture a bank where onboarding takes seconds, where credit adjusts daily, where fraud is predicted before it happens, and where customers interact through intelligent agents that know their preferences better than any relationship manager. Branches become service hubs, mobile apps fade into background APIs, and intelligence flows across borders as fast as money does. The bank of 2030 is already emerging—it just isn't evenly distributed yet.

"AI won't just change how banks operate. AI will change what a bank **is**."

"By 2030, the banks that thrive will not be the most digital—they will be the most intelligent."

Chapters 1–12 explained:

- the death of digital transformation
- the rise of AI as a core infrastructure
- the decision-centric architecture
- the operating model redesign
- generative AI and autonomous agents

- regulatory evolution
- organisational rewiring

Now we bring all of these threads together to describe the **endgame**:

What does a fully mature, AI-first bank look like by the year 2030?

This chapter paints the full vision.

We will cover:

1. The macro forces shaping banking 2030
2. The new AI-first competitive landscape
3. The 2030 AI bank architecture
4. The disappearance of traditional products
5. The emergence of "autonomous money systems"
6. AI-first credit, risk, identity and AML
7. Human–AI workforce design
8. AI-led compliance and real-time supervision
9. Bigtech, fintech and banking power shifts
10. The geopolitical dimensions of AI banking
11. The ultimate question: **Do banks survive? Or do they transform?**

1. The Macro Forces Driving the AI-First Bank of 2030

Simultaneous waves shape the world of 2030:

- generative AI
- autonomous agents
- real-time payments
- global KYC networks
- programmable money

- embedded finance
- digital identity
- behavioural risk modelling
- tokenised assets
- cross-border trade platforms
- SME ecosystems

Traditional boundaries between banks, fintechs, bigtechs and software companies dissolve.

1.1 Seven Forces Converging by 2030

1. **AI becomes infrastructure**

   Not a feature—a utility.

2. **Identity becomes behavioural**

   Devices, biometrics, behavioural signatures.

3. **Credit becomes adaptive**

   Continuous underwriting and instant capital.

4. **Risk becomes predictive**

   Models replace rules and committees.

5. **Compliance becomes autonomous**

   AI monitors everything in real time.

6. **CX becomes conversational**

   Apps shrink. Conversations dominate.

7. **Money becomes programmable**

   Instant, conditional, global.

(see Figure 13.1)

Figure 13.1 – The Seven Forces Shaping the 2030 Bank

AI Infra | Behavioural Identity | Adaptive Credit
Predictive Risk | Autonomous Compliance
Conversational CX | Programmable Money

2. The Competitive Landscape of 2030: The Four New Species of Banks

The "bank of 2030" will not be a single organism.

Instead, the financial ecosystem evolves into **four species**.

2.1 Species 1 – AI-First Banks

Incumbents that successfully:

- re-architect their cores
- build decision engines
- embrace LLM-driven operations
- adopt agent-based workflows

These banks compete on **intelligence**, not branches or apps.

2.2 Species 2 – Bigtech Finance Platforms

Amazon, Google, Apple, Alibaba, Tencent, Meta, Grab, Paytm.

They compete with:

- distribution
- data
- behavioural signals
- ecosystems

They integrate finance invisibly into lifestyle.

2.3 Species 3 – Autonomous Fintechs

Fintechs built natively on AI:

- plug-in credit
- agent-based lending
- self-optimising fraud systems
- autonomous wallets

They do not mimic banks.

They bypass them.

2.4 Species 4 – Infrastructure Champions

Cloud, API, and AI platform players:

- AWS
- Azure
- GCP
- Stripe
- Mambu
- Thought Machine
- AI model marketplaces

They power the intelligence layer.

(see Figure 13.2)

Figure 13.2 – The Four Species of 2030 Financial Institutions

```
AI-FIRST BANKS         | BIGTECH PLATFORMS
-----------------------|-----------------------
AUTONOMOUS FINTECHS    | INFRASTRUCTURE LAYERS
```

3. The Architecture of the AI-First Bank of 2030

By 2030, the bank's architecture will **no longer be account-centric.**

It becomes **decision-centric** and **intelligence-driven.**

The architecture has **five layers:**

1. **Real-time data mesh**
2. **Universal identity graph**
3. **Intelligence engine (AI + LLMs + Agents)**
4. **Programmable product systems**
5. **Human oversight and governance fabric**

(see Figure 13.3)

Figure 13.3 – The 2030 AI-First Bank Architecture

```
+------------------------------------------------------+
|            HUMAN OVERSIGHT LAYER                      |
+------------------------------------------------------+
|            INTELLIGENCE LAYER                         |
|  (AI Models + LLMs + Agents + Decision Engine)        |
+------------------------------------------------------+
|          UNIVERSAL IDENTITY GRAPH                     |
+------------------------------------------------------+
|            REAL-TIME DATA MESH                        |
+------------------------------------------------------+
|          PROGRAMMABLE PRODUCT LAYER                   |
+------------------------------------------------------+
```

4. Products Disappear – Systems Replace Products

By 2030, "products" as we know them will vanish.

4.1 Loans Become Streams of Capital

Continuously adjusted:

- credit limits
- pricing
- tenor
- exposure

4.2 Accounts Become Behaviour Containers

Your identity + behaviour = your account.

4.3 Cards Become Payment Instructions

Linked to:

- rules
- preferences
- context

4.4 Insurance Becomes Event-Driven

Triggered automatically by:

- location
- transactions
- device signals
- health indicators

4.5 Investments Become Automated Portfolios

AI curates based on:

- personality
- risk
- goals

- behaviour
- events

The customer no longer "chooses products".

The bank **configures personalised financial systems**.

5. Autonomous Money Systems: The New Consumer Reality

The most radical shift by 2030 is that money becomes:

- smart
- adaptive
- self-optimising
- rules-based
- agent-driven
- programmatically controlled

5.1 Examples

Example 1 – Auto-budgeting

Your wallet reassigns funds in real time.

Example 2 – Self-optimising savings

Agent moves funds between:

- deposits
- money market
- treasury bills
- crowdfunding
- investments

automatically.

Example 3 – Crisis response

If income drops:

- limits adjust
- pricing shifts
- instalments restructured

automatically.

Example 4 – Buying a home

AI agent:

- analyses income
- monitors housing market
- predicts interest rates
- identifies loan optimality
- triggers approval

6. AI-First Credit Systems of 2030

Credit evolves from:

- static decisions
- annual reviews
- rigid scorecards

to **continuous underwriting**.

6.1 Continuous Credit

The system monitors:

- cashflow
- sentiment

- transaction patterns
- network behaviour
- macro signals

This allows:

- daily limit changes
- dynamic pricing
- contextual approvals

6.2 Event-Driven Credit

Examples:

- salary delay → temporary extension
- travel → dynamic FX limits
- medical emergency → instant pre-approved financing

6.3 Behavioural Credit Graphs

Credit decisions use behavioural networks.

(see Figure 13.4)

Figure 13.4 – Behavioural Credit Graph (2030)

```
Customer
 |
 +--> Income Stability Cluster
 |
 +--> Transaction Behaviour Cluster
 |
 +--> Social/Network Trust Cluster
 |
 +--> Device and Identity Consistency Cluster
```

7. Predictive Risk and Algorithmic Stability

Risk in 2030 is:

- dynamic
- predictive
- network-aware
- real time

AI engines identify:

- micro-shifts in behaviour
- transaction anomalies
- liquidity risks
- sector shocks
- fraud waves
- geopolitical exposure

7.1 The 2030 Risk Control Tower

Risk teams monitor:

- model drift
- exposure clusters
- early-warning signals
- stress projections
- customer behaviour flows

(see Figure 13.5)

Figure 13.5 – AI-Driven Risk Control Tower

DATA STREAMS --> PREDICTIVE MODELS --> EARLY WARNINGS --> ACTIONS

8. Identity of 2030: Behaviour, Not Documents

Identity becomes:

- continuous
- multi-modal
- behavioural

Components include:

- biometrics
- device signatures
- behavioural patterns
- network position
- transaction DNA

8.1 Identity Graph

All identity signals converge into one unified graph.

(see Figure 13.6)

Figure 13.6 – The 2030 Identity Graph

+ Biometrics
+ Devices
+ Behaviour
+ Network Links
+ Location Patterns
+ Transaction DNA

↓

Unified Identity Graph

9. Autonomous Compliance: Machines Policing Machines

Compliance transforms from:

- document reviews
- retrospective audits
- rules-based alerts

to:

- real-time surveillance
- network-level AML
- predictive risk flagging
- autonomous false positive reduction

9.1 Autonomous AML

AI detects:

- mule accounts
- synthetic identities
- layered transactions
- obfuscated flows
- coordinated rings

9.2 Regulatory Reporting

Reports become:

- auto-generated
- real-time
- API-driven

Regulators receive:

- live dashboards
- model explanations

- behaviour patterns
- anomaly alerts

Compliance becomes **continuous**.

10. The Workforce of 2030: Humans and AI Working Side by Side

By 2030, every role is:

- augmented
- accelerated
- supported
- made more precise

10.1 Human Work

What humans specialise in:

- judgement
- ethics
- empathy
- complex negotiation
- human understanding
- strategy
- creativity
- governance

10.2 AI Work

What AI specialises in:

- summarising
- predicting

- drafting
- detecting
- explaining
- coaching
- reasoning

10.3 The New Banking Roles

New roles appear:

- AI supervisors
- Model governance officers
- Synthetic data engineers
- Agent orchestrators
- Behavioural risk modellers
- Prompt designers
- AI ethics stewards

Banks become **intelligent institutions powered by human–AI collaboration.**

11. Bigtech vs Banks: The Power Shift

By 2030, the lines blur.

11.1 Bigtech Advantages

- deeper data
- daily behavioural signals
- stronger ecosystems
- conversational dominance
- trust in user experience

11.2 Bank Advantages

- regulatory licence
- balance sheet
- risk orchestration
- financial trust

11.3 The Hybrid Future

Banks + Bigtech partnerships dominate.

Bigtech becomes:

- distribution
- interface
- ecosystem

Banks become:

- risk engines
- liquidity providers
- compliance guardians

(see Figure 13.7)

Figure 13.7 – The Hybrid Finance Model (2030)

BIGTECH → Distribution + Experience

BANKS → Balance Sheet + Risk

AI → Intelligence + Personalisation

12. Geopolitics of AI Banking: New Financial Power Structures

Nations with the best AI:

- win capital flows

- dominate AML monitoring
- reduce fraud
- attract fintech ecosystems

12.1 AI Becomes a National Advantage

Countries with:

- identity systems
- real-time payment rails
- progressive regulation
- AI-friendly compliance
- cross-border collaboration

lead global financial innovation.

12.2 Cross-Border Identity Networks

By 2030:

- identity is multi-country
- fraud detection is global
- AML is coordinated

Financial crime across borders collapses under AI intelligence nets.

13. Will Banks Survive 2030? Or Transform?

Banks do not die.

But the **banking model** dies.

What survives?

- decision engines
- capital orchestration

- risk governance
- compliance architecture
- identity infrastructure

What disappears?

- branches
- app-centric design
- static credit
- rigid products
- paper-based compliance
- human-only operations

The bank of 2030 is not a place you go.

It is a living financial intelligence that goes with you.

Conclusion: The AI-First Bank Is Inevitable – And Already Emerging

Everything in this chapter leads to a single truth:

The AI-First Bank of 2030 is not an institution.

It is an intelligent system.

A system that:

- senses
- thinks
- acts
- learns
- adapts

And it is built on:

- real-time data

- behavioural identity
- continuous credit
- predictive risk
- autonomous compliance
- conversational CX
- LLM-driven operations
- agent-driven workflows

The winners of 2030 will be:

- the most intelligent banks
- not the biggest
- not the oldest
- not the most digital

The winners of 2030 will be the banks with the best decision systems—accurate, adaptive, and fast.

"The bank with the best model will win. And the bank that thinks the fastest will own the future"

CHAPTER 14

AI-Native Product Design: How Banks Build Adaptive, Personalised, Self-Optimising Financial Systems (Not Products)

"Products were built for the digital age. Systems are built for the intelligence age."

This chapter explains why financial products must be re-engineered from the ground up for an intelligence-first world. It introduces new design principles where products are dynamic, adaptive, and behaviour-driven rather than static bundles. It outlines how banks can build AI-native offerings that sense context, adjust parameters automatically, and deliver personalised outcomes at scale.

Financial products were built for a world of static data, predictable behaviour, and slow decision cycles. That world is gone. Imagine designing products that adapt as customers change, learn from every interaction, and update themselves automatically. AI-native products are not bundles—they are dynamic systems that sense the user's life and respond in real time.

"Products were created for the distribution era. Systems are created for the intelligence era."

"AI-native product design does not start with features. It starts with behaviour, prediction, and evolution."

The shift from digital to AI-first banking is not only architectural or operational—it is fundamentally **product-driven**.

The concept of a "banking product"—card, account, loan, savings, overdraft—was invented for a world where banks controlled distribution.

But when:

- interfaces become conversational
- identity becomes behavioural
- credit becomes adaptive
- pricing becomes personalised
- risk becomes predictive
- journeys become autonomous
- money becomes programmable
- agents execute financial decisions

... the very idea of a product becomes obsolete.

This chapter explains how to design AI-native financial systems that:

- adapt
- personalise
- self-improve
- evolve dynamically
- anticipate customer needs
- reduce friction
- optimise financial outcomes

We cover:

1. The death of the traditional product
2. Behaviour-first product design
3. Prediction as the core product primitive
4. Adaptive credit systems
5. Dynamic deposit and saving ecosystems
6. Personalised pricing systems

7. Behaviour-driven insurance flows
8. Autonomous SME financial products
9. Programmable money and financial agents
10. The AI-native product design framework
11. The product pods and architecture for AI-first development
12. The endgame: self-optimising financial life systems

1. Why Traditional Banking Products Break in the AI Era

Traditional products are:

- static
- rigid
- rule-based
- predefined
- periodic
- human-configured

They assume:

- limited data
- delayed feedback
- manual underwriting
- human operations
- stable customer patterns

AI destroys these assumptions.

1.1 The Core Limitations of Traditional Products

Limitation 1 – Static configuration

A loan approved once does not adjust to new behaviour.

Limitation 2 – Fixed pricing

Rates rarely adjust to risk changes.

Limitation 3 – Manual underwriting

Slow. Expensive. Reactive.

Limitation 4 – One-size-fits-all segmentation

Customers are grouped based on blunt instruments.

Limitation 5 – No behavioural learning

Products do not evolve with usage.

1.2 The Digital Era Did Not Fix This

Digital channels only made **the old products faster**, not smarter.

What changed?

- onboarding
- distribution
- interfaces

What did not change?

- credit logic
- risk models
- pricing methods
- product design
- behaviour adaptation

1.3 AI Rewrites the Model

AI-native products:

- adapt to behaviour

- evolve with usage
- personalise based on signals
- update in real time
- optimise customer outcomes

This requires a new product philosophy.

2. Behaviour-First Product Design: The New Paradigm

In AI-native banking, the product does not start with:

- features
- limits
- pricing
- workflows

It starts with:

- behaviour
- prediction
- context
- patterns
- risk signatures
- intent signals

2.1 The Behaviour Stack

A behaviour-first product captures:

1. **Identity behaviour**

   Biometrics + device + usage patterns

2. **Financial behaviour**

   Spend patterns, incomes, obligations

3. **Network behaviour**

   Peer groups, merchants, locations

4. **Temporal behaviour**

   Time-based patterns, seasonality

5. **Emotional behaviour**

Extracted via LLM conversation

(see Figure 14.1)

Figure 14.1 – The Behaviour Stack for AI-Native Products

BEHAVIOUR =

Identity + Financial + Network + Temporal + Emotional

2.2 Behaviour Becomes the Interface

Instead of buttons and screens:

- the product observes
- the product predicts
- the product suggests
- the product adapts

2.3 A Product Is No Longer a Box – It Is a Brain

Every AI-native product becomes a feedback loop.

(see Figure 14.2)

Figure 14.2 – Product as an Intelligent Loop

SENSE --> PREDICT --> DECIDE --> ACT --> LEARN --> (back to SENSE)

3. Prediction Is the Core Product Primitive

In the digital world, products were built around:

- rules
- eligibility criteria
- fixed configurations

In the AI world, products are built around **predictions**.

3.1 Key Prediction Types

1. Creditworthiness prediction
2. Cashflow prediction
3. Fraud likelihood prediction
4. Churn prediction
5. Lifecycle prediction
6. Context prediction
7. Intent prediction
8. Profitability prediction
9. Risk prediction

3.2 Predictions Become Product Features

For example:

1. overdraft based on cashflow prediction
2. FX limit based on travel prediction
3. pricing based on profitability prediction
4. fraud checks based on behavioural prediction

Prediction is the new button.

4. Adaptive Credit Systems: Lending That Evolves Daily

Credit is the most powerful area of AI-native design.

4.1 Continuous Underwriting

Every customer receives:

- a dynamic limit
- updated daily
- based on behaviour

Traditional underwriting becomes obsolete.

4.2 Event-Driven Credit

Credit adjusts based on triggers:

- salary received → limit increases
- anomaly detected → limit decreases
- travel detected → FX credit activation
- emergency signals → instant emergency credit
- income fluctuation → dynamic restructuring

4.3 Behavioural Credit Graphs

Credit decisions use graph intelligence.

(see Figure 14.3)

Figure 14.3 – Behavioural Credit Graph

```
Income Node ------> Spend Node ------> Stability Node
 |          |           |
 +--> Personality Node ----> Risk Node---+
```

4.4 Personalised Loan Structures

Instead of:

- fixed EMIs
- fixed tenors
- fixed pricing

AI-native credit products offer:

- dynamic instalments
- flexible repayments
- adaptive tenors
- context-sensitive pricing

5. Dynamic Deposit and Savings Systems

Savings become:

- automated
- goal-linked
- behaviour-driven
- event-triggered

5.1 Intelligent Auto-Saving

The system predicts:

- upcoming expenses
- cashflow dips
- salary cycles

Then automatically:

- allocates savings

- adjusts goals
- moves funds
- optimises yield

5.2 Multi-Pocket Dynamic Accounts

Accounts contain dynamic pockets:

- emergency
- lifestyle
- travel
- investment
- goals

Each pocket self-manages.

6. Personalised Pricing Systems

Pricing evolves from:

- slabs
- tiers
- fixed rates

To:

- individualised curves
- behaviour-driven fees
- risk-aware APRs
- dynamic FX pricing
- usage-sensitive insurance premiums

6.1 AI Pricing Engine

The engine considers:

- behavioural risk
- cashflow patterns
- profitability potential
- loyalty markers
- network signals

(see Figure 14.4)

Figure 14.4 – AI Pricing System

DATA --> MODELS --> PRICE CURVE --> PERSONALISED RATE

7. Behaviour-Driven Insurance

Insurance becomes:

- usage-based
- pattern-driven
- sensor-informed
- AI-priced

7.1 Adaptive Coverage

Coverage changes with behaviour:

- driving patterns
- health indicators
- spending flows
- travel patterns

7.2 Instant Claims Processing

LLMs read:

- receipts
- images
- descriptions

AI:

- validates
- detects fraud
- predicts loss
- approves claims

8. Autonomous SME Product Systems

SMEs are perfect for AI-native design.

SMEs need:

- cashflow prediction
- invoice financing
- payroll support
- vendor payments
- inventory credit
- working capital cycles

8.1 The SME Autonomous Financial Engine

AI:

- predicts receivables
- flags risks

- suggests payments
- automates tax
- prepares compliance

8.2 Inventory-Based Credit

Credit based on:

- SKU movement
- seasonality
- purchase volume
- supplier network

8.3 Invoice Graph Risk

AI predicts:

- fraud
- invoice risk
- counterparty behaviour

9. Programmable Money and Financial Agents

By 2030, customers will interact with money as programmable flows.

9.1 Money With Conditions

You set rules:

- "Save 10% of all income."
- "Decline transactions after 11 pm."
- "If rent increases, adjust budget."
- "If salary delays, activate overdraft."

9.2 Autonomous Financial Agents

Agents:

- control payments
- restructure loans
- execute investments
- optimise taxes
- negotiate pricing
- plan cashflow

(see Figure 14.5)

Figure 14.5 – Autonomous Financial Agent

SENSE --> PREDICT --> PLAN --> EXECUTE --> REPORT

10. The AI-Native Product Design Framework

AI-first product teams use a new design framework:

Step 1 – Behaviour Mapping

Identify key:

- signals
- triggers
- intents

Step 2 – Prediction Modelling

Define:

- what predictions matter
- what signals feed them

Step 3 – Adaptive Logic

Determine:

- how the product evolves
- how it responds to prediction shifts

Step 4 – Personalisation Layer

Tie personalisation to:

- risk
- pricing
- credit
- features

Step 5 – Agent Integration

Add:

- workflows
- automation
- decision architecture

Step 6 – Compliance Guardrails

Define:

- limits
- boundaries
- human intervention

Step 7 – Feedback Loop Integration

How the product:

- learns
- improves
- retrains

(see Figure 14.6)

Figure 14.6 – AI-Native Product Design Loop

BEHAVIOUR → PREDICTION → ADAPTATION → PERSONALISATION → AGENTS → GUARDRAILS → FEEDBACK

11. The AI Product Pod: New Roles and Delivery Model

The AI-first product pod includes:

- Product Manager (AI-native)
- Behavioural Scientist
- Data Scientist
- ML Engineer
- Backend Engineer
- UX Designer
- Compliance Technologist
- Model Risk Analyst
- Agent Orchestrator

(see Figure 14.7)

Figure 14.7 – The AI Product Pod Structure

```
PRODUCT MANAGER
   |
   +--> Behaviour Scientist
   +--> Data Scientist
   +--> ML Engineer
   +--> Backend Engineer
   +--> UX Designer
   +--> Compliance Technologist
   +--> Model Risk Analyst
   +--> Agent Orchestrator
```

12. Endgame: The Customer's Financial Life Becomes Self-Optimising

The ultimate vision of AI-native product design is simple:

The bank becomes the customer's autonomous financial system.

12.1 The Self-Optimising Financial Life System

A single AI agent:

- monitors behaviour
- adjusts credit
- manages budgets
- optimises savings
- predicts risks
- negotiates pricing
- structures insurance
- automates tasks
- executes investment plans
- ensures compliance
- protects against fraud

(see Figure 14.8)

Figure 14.8 – The Self-Optimising Financial Life System

PLAN → PROTECT → OPTIMISE → EXECUTE → REVIEW → LEARN

12.2 The Bank Evolves Into Five Roles

By 2030, the AI-native bank will become:

1. **A financial operating system**
2. **A risk intelligence network**

3. **A behavioural identity hub**
4. **A capital orchestration engine**
5. **An autonomous financial agent for customers**

The product disappears.

The system remains.

Conclusion: AI-Native Product Design Is the Future of Banking

Traditional product design is incompatible with AI-first banking.

The new world requires:

- behaviour-first philosophy
- prediction-first design
- adaptive systems
- autonomous agents
- personalised pricing
- dynamic credit
- programmable money
- SME engines
- self-optimising personal finance

In the next chapter, we move from design to reach—how AI-native systems are embedded into platforms, marketplaces, and workflows so the bank becomes present wherever life and business happen.

"Products fade. Systems endure. Intelligence evolves."

CHAPTER 15

AI Distribution and Ecosystem Strategy

"In the future, customers won't come to banks. Banks will flow to customers."

This chapter examines how distribution shifts from channels to ecosystems and how AI turns embedded finance into a scalable, profitable distribution architecture. It explains the new mechanics and economics of acquisition, conversion, and retention when banking is delivered through APIs, agents, and workflow integrations rather than apps and branches.

Distribution once meant branches, ATMs, agents, call centres, and apps. In the AI era, distribution means something fundamentally different: being present at the precise moment a financial need emerges—inside the ecosystem where life and business already happen.

Customers will no longer "go to the bank" to borrow, pay, insure, or invest. Those decisions will surface inside commerce platforms, messaging threads, payroll systems, logistics networks, and digital marketplaces—triggered by context, powered by real-time risk, and executed through APIs and autonomous agents.

The winners of the next decade will not be the banks with the most channels. They will be the banks that flow into the right environments, at the right moment, with the right intelligent decision, often before the customer consciously asks.

"The bank of 2030 will not wait for customers to come to it. The bank will go wherever life and business happen."

"AI does not just transform products—it transforms distribution, embedding the bank into the fabric of digital society."

Digital banking attempted to bring everything into the bank's app.

AI-first banking inverts the paradigm:

The bank goes to the customer—anywhere, everywhere, invisibly.

This chapter explains how AI transforms the distribution layer of finance:

- platforms
- merchants
- e-commerce
- logistics
- supply chains
- mobility
- travel
- B2B marketplaces
- ERP systems
- payroll engines
- social platforms
- conversational interfaces
- superapps

The shift is profound:

- From branch → to app → to embedded → to ambient intelligence
- From distribution → to orchestration
- From channels → to ecosystems
- From selling financial products → to powering economic flows
- From transactional banking → to contextual finance

We cover:

1. Why AI rewrites distribution
2. The evolution from channels to ecosystems
3. The four layers of AI-first embedded banking

4. Consumer ecosystems
5. Merchant ecosystems
6. SME and supply chain ecosystems
7. B2B platforms and workflow banking
8. AI-driven distribution engines
9. Relationship managers augmented by AI
10. Autonomous ecosystem agents
11. Open finance + API intelligence
12. The economics of AI-first distribution
13. The 2030 ecosystem bank architecture
14. The risks, regulations and governance model
15. The endgame: ambient finance in a fully intelligent world

1. Why AI Rewrites Distribution

Traditional distribution is linear:

- branches
- call centres
- mobile apps
- websites
- agents

The digital era allowed:

- mobile onboarding
- digital journeys
- push notifications
- self-service tools

But **AI changes distribution fundamentally** because AI enables:

- context
- prediction
- autonomy
- personalisation
- embedded flows
- dynamic risk/credit/pricing
- real-time decisioning

1.1 Distribution Shifts From Place → to Presence

Traditional bank:

> "The customer comes to me."

Digital bank:

> "The customer uses my app."

AI-first bank:

> "I go where the customer already is."
>
> "I anticipate the need before the customer expresses it."
>
> "I embed myself into real-world ecosystems."

1.2 Distribution Becomes Intelligent

Distribution used to be "channels."

AI turns distribution into:

- an adaptive mesh
- a predictive orchestration layer
- an invisible intelligence network

(see Figure 15.1)

Figure 15.1 – Evolution of Distribution

BRANCH → APP → EMBEDDED → AMBIENT (AI-FIRST)

2. Channels → Ecosystems: The New Distribution Logic

Banks controls channels.

Customers control ecosystems.

People increasingly live inside:

- WhatsApp
- TikTok
- Instagram
- e-commerce marketplaces
- ride-hailing platforms
- SME apps
- accounting systems
- logistics platforms
- HR and payroll tools

Banks cannot expect customers to leave those environments to interact with them.

2.1 The Bank Must Integrate Into:

- lifestyle ecosystems
- commerce ecosystems
- work ecosystems
- enterprise ecosystems
- supply chain ecosystems

2.2 AI Enables This Integration

AI allows:

- real-time risk
- instant underwriting
- adaptive pricing
- behavioural identity
- embedded intelligence

This allows the bank to be **present inside ecosystems without friction**.

3. The Four Layers of AI-First Embedded Banking

AI-native embedded finance has four layers:

1. **Intelligence Layer** (risk, identity, pricing, prediction)
2. **Distribution Layer** (APIs, agents, SDKs, embeddings)
3. **Product Layer** (adaptive product systems)
4. **Ecosystem Layer** (platforms, merchants, SMEs, apps)

(see Figure 15.2)

Figure 15.2 – The Four Layers of AI-First Embedded Finance

```
+--------------------------+
|   ECOSYSTEM LAYER        |
+--------------------------+
|  PRODUCT SYSTEMS         |
+--------------------------+
|   DISTRIBUTION LAYER     |
+--------------------------+
| INTELLIGENCE LAYER       |
+--------------------------+
```

4. Consumer Ecosystems: Finance Where Life Happens

Consumers spend most of their time in:

- social platforms
- messaging apps
- e-commerce
- travel portals
- marketplaces
- ride-hailing apps
- food delivery apps

AI-native embedded finance integrates seamlessly into these flows.

4.1 Social Platforms (Meta, TikTok, Instagram, X)

Embedded finance becomes:

- one-click credit
- creator monetisation
- micro-lending
- instant payouts
- fraud alerts in chat
- AI-driven savings suggestions
- dynamic credit scoring based on creator earnings

LLMs understand:

- messages
- conversations
- voice notes

They respond:

- "Raj, your spending this week is 18% above average."
- "Shall I move $200 to savings?"
- "I detected duplicate subscriptions—cancel?"

This is ambient finance.

4.2 Messaging Platforms (WhatsApp, Telegram, WeChat)

Millions already use WhatsApp for:

- business
- sales
- customer service

AI-first banks embed:

- conversational onboarding
- instant credit offers
- small business financing
- fraud alerts
- RM agents
- FX calculators
- cashflow insights

The bank becomes a WhatsApp thread.

4.3 E-commerce Platforms (Amazon, Jumia, Lazada, Shopify)

AI-first embedded systems:

- score sellers in real time
- finance inventory instantly
- optimise pricing

- provide working capital loans
- insure shipments
- enable one-click credit at checkout

Example: One-Click Credit at Checkout

AI:

- checks behavioural risk
- checks income
- checks fraud signals
- makes decision
- sets personalised limits
- offers contextual payment plans
- Decision time: **< 200 milliseconds**

(see Figure 15.3)

Figure 15.3 – Embedded AI Credit at Checkout

CHECKOUT → RISK MODEL → PRICING MODEL → DECISION → OFFER

5. Merchant Ecosystems: AI-Driven Merchant Banking

Merchants need:

- payments
- working capital
- risk protection
- chargeback management
- settlement financing

AI-first banks embed services directly into:

- POS systems

- merchant dashboards
- payment gateways

5.1 Dynamic Merchant Credit

AI predicts:

- daily sales
- returns
- seasonality
- foot traffic
- marketplace ratings
- customer mix
- cashflow cycles

Credit adjusts automatically.

5.2 Real-Time Risk and Fraud Protection

Merchants receive:

- AI-driven fraud alerts
- chargeback prevention nudges
- anomaly detection
- counterfeit signal detection

5.3 Fee Personalisation

Pricing adjusts based on:

- risk
- loyalty
- behaviour

6. SME and Supply Chain Ecosystems

SMEs interact with:

- suppliers
- buyers
- distributors
- shippers
- accountants
- ERP
- logistics
- inventory systems

AI-native embedded finance integrates inside each.

6.1 Supply Chain Finance 2.0 (AI-Driven)

Traditional supply chain finance is:

- manual
- paperwork-heavy
- periodic
- relationship-driven

AI-first SCF is:

- continuous
- behavioural
- predictive
- automated

AI predicts:

- invoice validity

- counterparty reliability
- fraud risk
- payment probability
- seasonal patterns

Then adjusts:

- credit
- pricing
- risk controls
- payment terms

(see Figure 15.4)

Figure 15.4 – AI-Driven Supply Chain Finance

INVOICES → NETWORK GRAPH → BEHAVIOUR MODELS → FINANCE DECISION

6.2 ERP and Accounting Systems

Embedded finance inside ERP:

- automated invoice financing
- payroll loans
- vendor payments
- tax intelligence
- cashflow agents
- FX optimisation

The ERP becomes the bank.

7. B2B Platforms and Workflow Banking

AI-first banks embed inside:

- HR tools
- procurement systems
- gig-work marketplaces
- logistics systems
- construction management platforms

7.1 Examples

HR Platforms

- salary estimation
- payday loans
- benefits optimisation

Gig Platforms

- instant payouts
- automated tax deductions

Procurement Platforms

- purchase financing
- dynamic supplier credit

Workflow becomes banking.

Banking becomes workflow.

8. AI-Driven Distribution Engines

AI orchestrates where and when to distribute financial products.

The bank creates:

- risk API
- identity API
- pricing API

- credit API
- fraud API
- AML API
- agent workflows

Platforms integrate them.

8.1 Distribution Engine Capabilities

1. Context recognition
2. Offer ranking
3. Dynamic pricing
4. Flow underwriting
5. Eligibility prediction
6. CX personalisation
7. Interrupt minimisation
8. Channel routing

(see Figure 15.5)

Figure 15.5 – AI Distribution Engine Flow

CONTEXT → RISK → PRICING → DECISION → OROFFER → DELIVERY CHANNEL

9. Relationship Managers and AI: Augmented Human Distribution

In corporate and SME banking, RMs remain central.

AI augments RMs by:

- writing meeting notes
- summarising conversations
- generating proposals

- suggesting pricing
- analysing financials
- predicting churn
- identifying opportunities
- providing real-time insights

9.1 RM AI Copilot

Every RM has a copilot that:

- analyses their portfolio
- prioritises outreach
- predicts needs
- drafts emails
- suggests cross-sell
- highlights risks

(see Figure 15.6)

Figure 15.6 – RM Copilot Loop

DATA → INSIGHTS → SUGGESTIONS → EXECUTION → FEEDBACK

10. Autonomous Ecosystem Agents

The next step beyond embedded finance is **embedded agents**.

Agents:

- monitor ecosystem flows
- trigger underwriting
- adjust pricing
- alert RMs

- generate credit memos
- detect anomalies
- negotiate terms
- execute workflows

10.1 Example: Autonomous SME Agent

In a supply chain ecosystem, the agent:

- monitors orders
- predicts cashflow
- offers invoice financing
- executes payments
- notifies RM

11. Open Finance + API Intelligence

APIs enable distribution, but AI adds:

- personalisation
- scoring
- dynamic limits
- compliance interpretation
- value optimisation

11.1 Intelligent APIs

APIs enriched with AI:

- understand context
- adapt behaviour
- enforce dynamic policy
- ensure safety

This is the next evolution of open finance.

12. Economics of AI-First Distribution

AI-first embedded models are more profitable.

12.1 Lower CAC

Customers acquired through ecosystems:

- lower friction
- higher trust
- higher conversion

12.2 Higher LTV

Contextual finance is:

- timely
- relevant
- needed

12.3 Reduced Risk

Behaviour-driven risk:

- reduces defaults
- reduces fraud

12.4 Lower Operations Cost

LLMs reduce:

- back office
- RM workloads
- underwriting time

12.5 Higher Fee Revenue

Dynamic pricing increases yield.

13. Architecture of the 2030 Ecosystem Bank

(see Figure 15.7)

Figure 15.7 – The 2030 Ecosystem Bank Architecture

```
          PLATFORM PARTNERS
  +----------+----------+---------------+
  | ECOMM    | SME ERP  | SOCIAL        |
  +----------+----------+---------------+
        ↓ Integrations |

+---------------------------------------+
|       DISTRIBUTION INTELLIGENCE       |
| (Agents + Offers + Routing + Context) |
+---------------------------------------+
        ↓
+---------------------------------------+
|   AI PRODUCT SYSTEMS (Adaptive)       |
+---------------------------------------+
        ↓
+---------------------------------------+
|  CORE INTELLIGENCE (Risk, LLMs, AML)  |
+---------------------------------------+
        ↓
+---------------------------------------+
|      DATA & IDENTITY GRAPH            |
+---------------------------------------+
```

14. Risks and Regulatory Considerations

AI-first distribution creates new regulatory risks:

14.1 Partner Risk

Banks rely on platform integrity.

14.2 Consumer Transparency

Customers must know:

- who is offering the financial product
- how decisions are made

14.3 Fair Pricing

AI dynamic pricing must avoid:

- discrimination
- opaque reasoning

14.4 LLM Safety

LLM interactions must be:

- safe
- auditable
- controlled

14.5 Data Sharing Consents

Must be:

- explicit
- revocable
- logged

15. Endgame: Ambient Finance

The ultimate vision:

- finance flows automatically
- credit activates proactively
- risk adjusts continuously
- pricing adapts naturally
- agents manage financial life

Finance becomes an ambient layer of life:

- invisible
- intelligent
- responsive

(see Figure 15.8)

Figure 15.8 – Ambient Finance Loop

LIVE → SIGNAL → PREDICT → ACT → ADJUST → LIVE

Conclusion: AI Turns Distribution Into a Living Ecosystem

The future bank:

- does not wait for customers
- embeds itself in life
- responds to context
- adapts to behaviour
- anticipates needs
- automates flows
- personalises solutions

- drives ecosystems
- becomes ambient

AI changes distribution just as radically as it changes products.

As distribution becomes ambient, treasury must become predictive, because liquidity now has to move as intelligently as customer demand. In Chapter Sixteen, we examine AI-First Treasury, Liquidity Optimisation and Market Intelligence: the next frontier where banks gain advantage through predictive liquidity, market sensing, and autonomous treasury operations.

"Banks will not compete for customers. They will compete for the places where customers live their lives."

CHAPTER 16

AI-First Treasury, Liquidity Optimisation and Market Intelligence

"Treasury stops looking backwards when intelligence helps it see forwards."

This chapter explores how AI transforms treasury from a backwards-looking, report-driven function into a predictive intelligence hub. It covers liquidity forecasting, stress simulations, hedging automation, capital optimisation, and real-time balance sheet steering. Treasury evolves from reconciling yesterday to anticipating tomorrow.

In the embedded, ecosystem-driven bank, liquidity no longer behaves like a slow-moving balance sheet variable. It behaves like a real-time signal—spiking with marketplace campaigns, shifting with payroll cycles, swinging with instant credit activation, and reacting to macro shocks in minutes, not weeks.

Traditional treasury was built for end-of-day views and committee rhythms. But when distribution becomes ambient, treasury must become predictive. AI transforms treasury from a backwards-looking reporting function into a live control tower that senses liquidity in motion, forecasts stress before it appears, automates hedging and funding actions, and continuously optimises balance sheet performance under clear governance guardrails.

"Treasury is the brainstem of the bank. AI turns it from reactive and spreadsheet-driven to predictive, automated, and self-correcting."

"By 2030, treasury and ALM will operate like an air-traffic control tower—continuously sensing, predicting, and balancing risk flows across the entire institution."

Digital transformation modernised channels.

AI transformation modernises **control**.

In most banks, treasury remains:

- Excel-intensive
- Manual
- Committee-driven
- Human judgement-heavy
- Dependent on periodic reporting
- Siloed from product, credit, risk, and liquidity systems

AI changes all of this.

This chapter explains **how AI rewrites Treasury, Liquidity, ALM, FTP (Funds Transfer Pricing), and Balance Sheet Management** across retail, SME, corporate, and wholesale banking.

We cover:

1. The structural weaknesses of traditional treasury
2. The 5-Layer AI Treasury Operating System
3. Real-time liquidity intelligence
4. Predictive ALM for interest-rate risk and liquidity shocks
5. Autonomous FTP and behavioural analytics
6. Intraday liquidity optimisation using AI + graph analytics
7. AI-native funding strategy
8. Stress-testing and scenario engines
9. LLMs for treasury operations
10. Treasury control tower of 2030
11. AI-driven capital optimisation (RWA, pricing, profitability)
12. How AI integrates treasury with risk, credit, fraud and compliance
13. Endgame: The Autonomous Balance Sheet

1. Why Traditional Treasury Models Fail in the AI Era

Treasury is the institution's:

- balance-sheet guardian
- liquidity controller
- interest-rate risk manager
- funding strategist
- capital allocator

But most treasuries still operate like it's 2005.

1.1 The Structural Problems

Problem 1: Periodic, not continuous

Liquidity is monitored:

- daily
- weekly
- monthly

Not **in real time.**

Problem 2: Data fragmentation

Critical data sits across:

- core banking
- lending systems
- card systems
- risk engines
- payments
- treasury management systems
- market data feeds

Problem 3: Excel-heavy stress testing

Scenario modelling is slow, manual, and backwards-looking.

Problem 4: FTP (Funds Transfer Pricing) is static

Pricing does not reflect real-time:

- risk
- duration
- behavioural forecasts

Problem 5: Behaviour is misunderstood

Traditional ALM assumes:

- fixed deposit durations
- fixed prepayment rates
- fixed liquidity runoff

  Which is not true.

  Behaviour varies by:

- seasonality
- customer type
- device usage
- transaction patterns

AI rewrites these assumptions.

2. The 5-Layer AI Treasury Operating System

(Hybrid technical + strategic; Retail + SME + Corporate + Wholesale)

Everything in AI-first treasury sits inside this framework.

(see Figure 16.1)

Figure 16.1 – Five-Layer AI Treasury Operating System

```
+------------------------------------------------------------+
| LAYER 5: TREASURY CONTROL TOWER (AUTONOMOUS ACTION) |
+------------------------------------------------------------+
| LAYER 4: DECISION & OPTIMISATION ENGINE                    |
+------------------------------------------------------------+
| LAYER 3: PREDICTIVE MODELS & SIMULATION                    |
+------------------------------------------------------------+
| LAYER 2: REAL-TIME SIGNALS & DATA MESH                     |
+------------------------------------------------------------+
| LAYER 1: SOURCE SYSTEMS (CBS, cards, payments, etc.)       |
+------------------------------------------------------------+
```

Layer 1 – Source Systems (Foundation Layer)

Treasury consumes data from all banking systems:

- Core banking (balances, maturities, flows)
- Payments (in/out flows)
- Lending systems (loan schedules)
- Cards (spend patterns)
- Market systems (FX, rates)
- Risk systems (PD, LGD, EAD)
- Trade finance platforms
- Corporate treasury portals

Treasury finally becomes connected to the **real bank**.

Layer 2 – Real-Time Signals and Data Mesh

Traditional treasury uses historical snapshots.

AI treasury uses **live signals**.

2.1 Types of Signals Collected

1. **Liquidity Signals**
    - Inflows/outflows
    - O/N balances
    - Intraday peaks
    - FX settlements
    - Card settlement patterns
2. **Behavioural Signals**
    - Withdrawal patterns
    - Prepayment indicators
    - Dormancy signals
    - Early-risk signs
    - Merchant flows (SME)
3. **Market Intelligence**
    - interest-rate curves
    - swap volatility
    - yield spreads
    - macroeconomic indicators
4. **Network/Graph Signals**

    Treasury uses graph analytics to identify:

    - liquidity dependencies
    - correlated exposures
    - network contagion risks

(see Figure 16.2)

Figure 16.2 – Treasury Behavioural Graph

```
Deposit Node → Withdrawal Cluster → Salary Pattern → Liquidity Risk Node
        |                |          |
        |                v          +→ FX Risk Node
        |            Behaviour Shifts
        |
        +→ Corporate Payments Cluster
```

Layer 3 – Predictive Models and Simulation Engines

This is where treasury becomes predictive.

AI Models Treasury Uses

3.1 Cashflow Forecasting Models

Predict inflows/outflows for:

- retail customers
- SMEs
- corporates

Across:

- daily
- weekly
- seasonal
- event-driven patterns

3.2 Behavioural Model Suite

Including:

- deposit runoff prediction
- early prepayment prediction

- loan behavioural models
- liquidity stickiness

3.3 Market Risk Models

- interest-rate risk
- FX risk
- yield curve projections

3.4 Liquidity Stress Models

AI runs:

- 1,000+ intraday scenarios
- overnight liquidity shocks
- corporate concentration risks

3.5 Contagion Graph Models

Predict systemic liquidity vulnerabilities.

(see Figure 16.3)

Figure 16.3 – AI Treasury Predictive Model Universe

```
Cashflow AI    Behaviour AI    ALM AI    Market AI
 |         |        |       |
 +---------------+---------------+------------+
          ↓
   Simulation Engine
```

Layer 4 – Decision and Optimisation Engine

This is the brain.

AI optimises:

- liquidity buffers
- funding mix
- pricing of deposits
- loan pricing
- hedging strategies
- FX positioning
- intraday liquidity usage
- capital allocation
- FTP (Funds Transfer Pricing)

4.1 Optimisation Objectives

The bank targets:

- regulatory liquidity ratios
- net interest income stability
- profitability
- capital efficiency
- liquidity risk appetite
- interest-rate risk appetite

4.2 Decision Engine Flow

(see Figure 16.4)

Figure 16.4 – Treasury Decision Engine Flow

FORECASTS --> OPTIMISE --> GENERATE ACTIONS --> CHECK GOVERNANCE --> EXECUTE

Layer 5 – The Treasury Control Tower (Autonomous)

Here, execution becomes:

- semi-automated
- under human supervision
- consistently optimised
- real-time

5.1 The Control Tower Does

- intraday liquidity balancing
- hedge execution
- FTP adjustments
- behavioural pricing
- contingency funding triggers
- capital optimisation
- scenario recalibration

Treasury evolves from:

- spreadsheet room → **intelligence room**
- monthly review → **continuous optimisation**
- manually reactive → **autonomously predictive**

3. Real-Time Liquidity Intelligence (Retail + SME + Corporate)

Most liquidity models assume patterns.

AI observes actual behaviour.

3.1 Retail Banking Liquidity

AI detects:

- salary cycles
- seasonal withdrawal patterns
- digital wallet transfers
- bill-payment flows

3.2 SME Liquidity

AI tracks:

- invoicing patterns
- supplier cycles
- payroll events
- tax timing

3.3 Corporate Liquidity

AI models:

- treasury sweep patterns
- FX settlements
- cross-border payment flows
- concentration risk

4. Predictive ALM: From Static Gap Analysis to Dynamic, Real-Time IRRBB Management

Traditional ALM uses:

- static maturity ladders
- interest-rate shock scenarios
- duration analysis

AI-first ALM uses:

- neural yield curve prediction
- behavioural repricing models
- dynamic interest-rate risk simulation

4.1 The ALM Engine of 2030

(see Figure 16.5)

Figure 18.5 – AI ALM Architecture

```
YIELD CURVE MODELS
     |
BEHAVIOUR MODELS --> REPRICING ENGINE --> NII SIMULATOR -->
ACTIONS
     |
CREDIT MODELS
```

4.2 NII (Net Interest Income) Optimisation

AI balances:

- deposit pricing
- loan pricing
- hedging
- balance-sheet structure

Automatically generating **NII-optimised lending strategy.**

5. Autonomous FTP (Funds Transfer Pricing)

FTP is broken in most banks:

- static
- slow

- opaque
- manually adjusted

AI turns FTP into a **dynamic intelligence system**.

5.1 AI-Based FTP Inputs

- behavioural duration
- liquidity premium
- risk premium
- intraday liquidity usage
- capital consumption
- stress contributions
- FX exposure

5.2 FTP Adjusts in Real-Time

Example:

- SME inflows spike → FTP lowers funding cost
- corporate withdrawals rise → FTP increases liquidity premium

Pricing finally becomes **scientific**.

6. Intraday Liquidity Optimisation (with Graph Engines)

Legacy banks manage liquidity on an end-of-day basis.

AI-first banks manage it **intraday**, continuously.

6.1 Graph Analytics for Payment Flows

AI maps:

- nodes (accounts, merchants, corporates)

- edges (money flows)
- volumes
- time-of-day patterns
- currency dependencies

(see Figure 16.6)

Figure 16.6 – Intraday Liquidity Graph

```
Corporate A → Bank Node → Clearing House → FX Node
     |           |           |           |
     v           + → SME Cluster -------> Retail Node
Salary Flows                    Payment Outflows
```

6.2 Intraday Liquidity Use Cases

- pre-funding decisions
- collateral allocation
- settlement risk prediction
- LCR/NSFR optimisation

7. AI-Native Funding Strategy

AI optimises:

- wholesale funding
- retail deposit strategy
- market borrowing
- bond issuance timing
- FX funding

7.1 AI Predicts Funding Costs

Using:

- yield trends
- cross-currency spreads
- macro indicators
- behaviour of competitor banks

AI suggests:

- "Issue a 3-year bond this week."
- "Increase tenor of wholesale funding."
- "Lower retail deposit pricing in segment X."

8. Stress-Testing and Scenario Engines

Traditional:

- annual
- template-based
- regulatory-driven

AI-first:

- continuous
- behaviour-based
- scenario-rich

8.1 Scenario Engine Types

- rate hikes
- liquidity shocks
- corporate defaults
- FX volatility
- fraud attack cascades
- geopolitical events

8.2 Autonomous Stress Testing

AI runs thousands of scenarios **daily**, alerting treasury in real time.

9. LLMs in Treasury: Cognitive Automation

LLMs transform treasury operations:

9.1 LLM Assistants Perform

- liquidity report drafting
- NII forecasting explanations
- hedging rationale summaries
- market commentary intelligence
- regulatory filings
- board pack preparation

9.2 LLM Agents Execute

- query market data
- summarise risk indicators
- validate hedging strategies
- write FTP policy updates

Treasury becomes a **cognitive powerhouse**.

10. The Treasury Control Tower of 2030

A single interface shows:

- live liquidity
- risk positions
- hedges

- funding mix
- FTP impacts
- stress results
- behavioural shifts

(see Figure 16.7)

Figure 18.7 – Treasury Control Tower

LIQUIDITY | NII | FTP | FUNDING | RISK | STRESS | BEHAVIOUR | ACTIONS

Treasury shifts from:

- reporting → **decisioning**
- analysing → **anticipating**
- managing → **optimising**

11. AI-Driven Capital Optimisation

AI helps optimise:

- RWA
- capital buffers
- allocation across businesses
- pricing based on capital usage

11.1 Capital Intelligence Engine

- links PD/LGD/EAD with capital consumption
- predicts tail risks
- identifies capital inefficiencies

11.2 RWA-Aware Product Design

Products get priced according to:

- risk
- liquidity
- duration

12. AI Treasury Integration With Risk, Fraud, Credit and AML

Treasury finally becomes connected to:

- Risk → PD models influence capital
- Credit → behavioural lending changes liquidity
- Fraud → fraud bursts increase outflows
- AML → blocked accounts affect inflows/outflows

AI unifies the bank.

13. The Autonomous Balance Sheet (Endgame)

The future is simple:

The balance sheet will manage itself.

Humans supervise.

AI executes.

13.1 Autonomous Functions

- liquidity balancing
- hedge execution
- pricing
- funding mix
- stress reactions
- capital allocation

13.2 Human Oversight

- ethical reasoning
- boundary setting
- crisis management
- strategic direction

AI does everything else.

Conclusion: Treasury Is the Final Frontier of AI Transformation

Treasury is:

- the foundation of the bank
- the oldest part of banking
- the most conservative function

But AI transforms it into:

- real-time
- predictive
- behaviour-driven
- liquidity-intelligent
- capital-optimised
- agent-enabled
- autonomously balanced

No AI-first bank is complete without an **AI-first treasury**.

In an ecosystem-first bank, liquidity moves at machine speed, and so does financial crime.

As real-time payments, instant credit, and cross-border flows accelerate, fraud and money laundering also become faster, more coordinated, and more adaptive.

In Chapter Seventeen, we move from balance-sheet intelligence to financial crime intelligence—building an AI-first Fraud and AML operating system that senses behavioural signals, maps networks, predicts typologies, and executes controls in real time under strong governance.

"In an AI future, liquidity is not managed—it is anticipated."

CHAPTER 17

Ai-First Fraud And Aml: A 5-Layer Intelligence Operating System For Retail, Sme And Corporate Banking

"Fraud is a network problem. Intelligence must be a network solution."

This chapter analyses why fraud and AML threats are becoming more complex, connected, and intelligent and why traditional rule-based systems fail to keep pace. It introduces the concept of networked intelligence for fraud, where banks collectively share patterns, signals, and behaviours. AI becomes the foundation for detecting synthetic identities, mule networks, cross-border flows, and next-gen financial crime.

Fraudsters no longer work alone; they operate in coordinated, AI-enhanced networks that adapt faster than traditional controls can respond. Banks must fight networks with networks. Imagine a system where institutions share behavioural signals, where synthetic identities are flagged by pattern recognition, and where AML alerts are generated before suspicious activity even occurs. Fraud becomes a real-time intelligence war.

Fraud Is No Longer a Transaction Problem—It Is a Network Intelligence Problem

Fraud has evolved faster than any other domain in banking.

Digital transformation:

- increased speed
- increased access
- increased digital volume
- expanded attack surfaces

But AI has transformed fraud itself.

Fraudsters now use:

- generative AI
- deepfakes
- synthetic identities
- bot farms
- scripted attacks
- automated credential stuffing
- hyper-scalable scam operations

At the same time, regulatory pressure on AML has intensified.

Banks are fined billions annually because:

- rules fail
- false positives overwhelm teams
- investigations are manual
- typologies are outdated
- money launderers operate across borders
- criminal networks exploit gaps between institutions

Traditional fraud and AML systems are:

- rule-based
- reactive
- siloed
- transaction-centric
- slow
- manually overloaded

The AI-first era demands a complete redesign.

This chapter introduces a **5-Layer AI Fraud and AML Operating System**, built for:

- retail banking
- SME banking
- corporate banking
- payment companies
- cross-border flows
- digital wallets
- FX and trade finance
- merchant acquiring

1. The 5-Layer AI Fraud and AML Operating System

This chapter introduces a **5-Layer AI Fraud and AML Operating System** for:

- Retail banking
- SME banking
- Corporate banking
- Payment companies and wallets
- Cross-border flows, FX, trade finance
- Merchant acquiring and marketplaces

1.1 The Operating Model

Layer 1 – Risk Sensing (Signals and Telemetry)

Layer 2 – Risk Prediction (Models, Graphs and Typologies)

Layer 3 – Risk Decisions (Real-Time Decision Engine)

Layer 4 – Risk Execution (Actions, Challenges, Escalations)

Layer 5 – Risk Learning (Feedback, Drift, Retraining)

Figure 17.1 – The 5-Layer AI Fraud and AML Operating System

```
+------------------------------+
| LAYER 5: LEARNING            |
+------------------------------+
| LAYER 4: ACTION              |
+------------------------------+
| LAYER 3: DECISION            |
+------------------------------+
| LAYER 2: PREDICTION          |
+------------------------------+
| LAYER 1: SIGNALS             |
+------------------------------+
```

2. Layer 1 – Risk Sensing

Risk sensing is the foundation. Fraud and AML cannot be intelligent unless the bank collects high-resolution signals across every surface. Traditional collection (transaction data + documents + basic KYC) is insufficient.

2.1 The Seven Signal Categories (Retail + SME + Corporate)

1. **Identity signals** (biometrics, liveness, doc authenticity, registry validation, UBO signals, entity resolution)
2. **Device signals** (device fingerprint, emulator detection, behavioural biometrics, app integrity)
3. **Network signals** (IP/VPN/TOR, merchant networks, account/device clusters, mule rings)
4. **Behavioural signals** (timing, navigation, velocity, patterns, salary cycle behaviour, deviations)
5. **Transaction signals** (structuring, layering patterns, geolocation mismatch, round-tripping, MCC shifts)
6. **Relationship signals** (customers, merchants, suppliers, counterparties, beneficial owners, nested networks)

7. **External intelligence** (sanctions/PEP, adverse media, cyber intel, consortium data, typology updates)

Why Layer 1 is Critical

Fraud and AML accuracy = breadth of signals × depth of context.

(see Figure 17.2)

Figure 17.2 – Network Signals in AI Fraud Detection

```
Account A ---- Device X ---- IP Z
 |          |          |
 + → Account B + → Device Y + → Merchant Q
```

3. Layer 2 – Risk Prediction

Layer 2 transforms raw signals into predictive intelligence using ML models, graph databases, anomaly engines, typology AI, embeddings, entity linking, and behavioural clustering.

3.1 Ml Model Suite (by use case)

- **Classification models** (fraud yes/no, AML suspicion, risky merchant, genuine login)
- **Regression models** (fraud probability, expected loss, risk score)
- **Sequence/temporal models** (structuring, layering, mule flows, behavioural drift)

3.2 Behavioural Graphs (Network Intelligence, not Transaction Checks)

Graph engines identify rings, collusion, identity clusters, and hidden relationships.

(see Figure 17.3)

Figure 17.3 – Behavioural Fraud Graph

```
Customer A → Device X → Merchant K
          |
    Customer C → IP Y
          |
    Merchant Z → Supplier M
```

3.3 Entity Resolution (Truth Layer For Identity)

Link accounts, directors, devices, phone/email/address/merchant relationships to detect synthetic identities.

3.4 Anomaly Detection (Zero-Day Readiness)

Isolation Forest, Autoencoders, one-class models, GNN anomalies.

3.5 AML Typology Models

Detect structuring, mule flows, rapid layering, circular flows, merchant collusion, invoice manipulation, shell networks.

3.6 Vector Embeddings + LLM Intelligence

Narrative analysis for SARs/STRs, adverse media interpretation, contextual merchant risk, document intelligence, conversational scam detection.

3.7 Layer 2 Outputs

Risk score, graph risk, entity confidence, anomaly confidence, typology matches, narrative risk → feeds Layer 3.

4. Layer 3 – Real-Time Risk Decisions

Layer 3 converts predictions into decisions. It must operate at machine speed, combine AI + policy, remain explainable, and support human oversight.

4.1 Decision Engine Architecture

Figure 17.4 – Real-Time Risk Decision Engine

```
REQUEST
 |
FEATURE LOOKUP
 |
MODEL SCORES (AI)
 |
POLICY GUARDRAILS (Rules)
 |
DECISION ORCHESTRATION
 |
ACTION OUTPUT
```

4.2 The Real-Time Decision Pipeline (Detailed)

- Request broker
- Feature fetcher (vector DB / graph DB / feature store / device store / profile store)
- Model router (fraud / AML / identity / sanctions / UBO / merchant)
- Rules overlay (regulatory hard stops + policy thresholds)
- Fused score engine (ensembles + consensus)
- Decision engine (approve/challenge/block/escalate)
- Explainability output + logging

(see Figure 17.5)

Figure 17.5 – Decision Pipeline Architecture

REQUEST

↓

FEATURE FETCHER ↓ VECTOR DB / GRAPH DB / FEATURE STORE

↓

MODEL ROUTER ↓ (Fraud / AML / Identity / Sanctions Models)

↓

RULES OVERLAY

↓

FUSED SCORE ENGINE

↓

DECISION ENGINE

↓

OUTCOME (approve / challenge / block / escalate / SAR)

4.3 Core Decision Types (7)

1. Approve
2. Approve with monitoring
3. Step-up authentication
4. Challenge (incl. LLM conversation)
5. Delay (for AML verification/data fetch)
6. Decline
7. Escalate (Human-in-the-loop)

4.4 Risk Tiers

Low → auto approve

Medium → challenge

High → decline

Severe → freeze + escalate

4.5 Behavioural Fusion (Multi-Model Consensus)

Graph + transformer/sequence + tabular ML + rules + LLM reasoning.

4.6 Corporate Decisioning Specifics

Payroll runs, treasury swings, vendor payments, SWIFT rails, approvals, seasonality, supplier networks, UBO chains.

4.7 Explainability (XAI) and Auditability

Top features, graph contributors, anomaly rationale, lineage, sanctions justification, counterparty relationship.

4.8 Human-in-the-loop Boundaries

Conflicting models, low confidence, high-value corporate transfers, sanctions partial matches, ambiguous typologies.

5. Layer 4 – Execution and Response Automation

Execution is operational muscle: actions, workflows, case creation, customer comms, rail integrations.

5.1 Execution Categories

- Transaction actions (approve/block/hold/reverse/refund)

- Identity actions (re-auth, biometric challenge, device re-bind, KYC refresh)
- Account actions (freeze/restrict/limit changes)
- AML actions (case creation, doc requests, SAR/STR drafting, approvals)
- Customer communication (LLM-driven notifications)
- Corporate actions (CFO override workflows, vendor authenticity checks)

5.2 AI Case Management Orchestration

Auto-generated case context, graph snapshots, device forensics, LLM summary, AI prioritisation.

(see Figure 17.6)

Figure 17.6 – AI Case Creation Workflow

Decision Engine

↓

CASE GENERATOR

↓

- • LLM Summary
- • Graph Snapshot
- • Features
- • Customer Timeline
- • Device Data

↓

ASSIGNED QUEUE

↓

INVESTIGATOR (HITL)

↓

FINAL ACTION

5.3 Autonomous Fraud Response

Velocity throttling, dynamic MFA, temporary limits, merchant-category locks, device revocation.

5.4 Automated AML Typology Execution

Smurfing → cluster freeze

Mule → network quarantine

Layering → escalate L2

Structuring → fragmentation alert

5.5 Payment Rail Integration

SWIFT, SEPA, ACH, RTP, PIX, ISO20022, card networks, mobile money.

Requirements: low latency, HA, in-flight modification, safe fallbacks.

5.6 Crisis Response Orchestration

Retail: PAN rotation, malware enforcement, phishing mass notifications

SME: vendor scam category blocks, invoice anomaly workflows

Corporate: vendor payment freezes, CFO-level alerts

6. Layer 5 – Continuous Learning and Evolution

Layer 5 makes the system self-improving, bounded by governance.

6.1 Feedback Sources

Outcomes, analyst actions, customer feedback, graph mutation tracking, drift detection, false positives/negatives, typology updates.

Figure 17.7 – Continuous Learning Loop

```
EVENTS → MODELS → DECISIONS → OUTCOMES
 ↑                 ↓
 ←--------- FEEDBACK ---------
```

6.2 Drift Detection And Self-Healing

Data drift, concept drift, attack drift, seasonal drift.

Self-healing: threshold tuning, confidence calibration, ensemble fallback, cluster relearning.

6.3 Zero-day Threats (Pattern Mutation)

Synthetic identity, mule farms, RATs, BEC, deepfake takeovers, adversarial attacks.

6.4 AML Typology Evolution

Clustering + anomaly detection + LLM narrative extraction + UBO recalibration.

6.5 Analyst–model Feedback Integration

Analyst decisions feed labels, reweighting, new signal creation; LLMs mine case notes for patterns.

6.6 Real-time vs Batch Learning

Fraud: real-time learning dominant

AML: hybrid (graph + sanctions + jurisdiction risk updates)

6.7 Governance for Continuous Learning

Approval gates, audit trails, override tracking, retraining logs, explainability standards.

7. Enterprise Fraud and AML Control Tower (EFCT)

The EFCT is the "war room" for unified oversight: real-time dashboards, attack heatmaps, cluster shifts, sanctions updates, model performance, case load, corporate wire risk, SME invoice risk.

7.1 Core Panels

Threat landscape, graph clusters, live sanctions, model health, case volumes, corporate wire anomalies, SME vendor graph, retail CNP heatmap.

(see Figure 17.8)

Figure 17.8 – EFCT High-Level Architecture

DATA PIPELINES

↓

AI MODELS →GRAPH ENGINE → LLM ENGINE

↓

RISK FUSION LAYER

↓

EFCT DASHBOARDS & ALERTS

↓

RISK OPS / EXCO / REGULATORS

7.2 Corporate Threat Zones

BEC, invoice fraud, treasury manipulation, vendor compromise, sanctions-sensitive trade.

7.3 SME Focus Zones

Fake vendors, fake invoices, collusion patterns, mule cashflow networks.

7.4 Retail Fraud Focus Zones

Phishing, malware, social engineering, card testing rings, mule accounts, compromised devices.

8. Regulatory Alignment in the AI-First Era

Regulators shift toward continuous AML, model governance, explainability, privacy controls, sanctions automation, cross-border information sharing.

Frameworks to map against (examples): EU AI Act, MAS FEAT, HKMA, OCC/Fed model risk, FCA responsible AI expectations, FATF digital identity guidance.

9. Future State: The Fraud and AML System of 2030

Autonomous, predictive, network-native, LLM-augmented, self-evolving.

9.1 Characteristics

Real-time detection, network graph intelligence, self-healing models, proactive containment, instant sanctions adaptation, behavioural biometrics.

9.2 AI-powered Threats

Deepfake voices, synthetic identities, AI phishing, AI-generated invoices, impersonation, adversarial attacks.

9.3 Autonomous Financial Crime Operations

Autonomous blocking, autonomous escalation, autonomous SAR drafting, autonomous recovery flows—humans supervise.

10. Conclusion: The New Risk Arms Race

Fraudsters evolve. Networks evolve. Typologies evolve. Only banks that evolve faster survive.

The 5-Layer AI Fraud and AML Operating System turns the bank into:

- a sensing organism
- a predictive machine

- a fast decision engine
- an execution powerhouse
- a self-learning intelligence

In Chapter Eighteen, we widen the lens from financial crime to the full risk universe—credit, market, liquidity, operational, cyber and model risk and show how AI turns risk into a real-time sensing, decisioning and learning organism across the entire bank.

"Fraud is no longer an attack. It is a pattern. And patterns are no match for intelligence."

CHAPTER 18

The Ai-Native Risk Function: How Banks Sense, Predict, Decide, Execute And Learn Risk In Real Time

"Risk advantage is no longer about protection; it is about prediction."

Here, the risk function is reimagined as an intelligence engine that continuously scans for threats, predicts exposures, and adapts controls automatically. The chapter contrasts traditional risk governance with dynamic, model-driven risk frameworks that operate at machine speed. It shows how AI-native risk functions become strategic assets, enabling growth with confidence rather than slowing it down.

Walk into a traditional risk department, and you'll see binders, policies, spreadsheets, and committees. Walk into an AI-native risk function, and you'll see live dashboards, model pipelines, stress simulations, anomaly maps, and self-learning detection systems. Risk becomes an active organism—continuously scanning, predicting, adjusting, and steering the institution toward resilience in real time.

"Risk in the AI-era banking is not measured. It is sensed."

"The bank of the future does not detect risk—it anticipates it."

"In real-time institutions, risk is not a function. It is an intelligent organism."

For 50 years, bank risk management was built on models, committees, governance, and backwards-looking metrics.

But as banking enters the intelligence era, this model collapses.

The traditional risk function was:

- periodic
- document-driven

- reactive
- human-led
- siloed
- past-oriented

The AI-native risk function is:

- continuous
- data-driven
- predictive
- autonomous
- interconnected
- future-oriented

This chapter explains how banks transform the entire risk universe—credit risk, market risk, liquidity risk, operational risk, fraud risk, conduct risk, compliance risk, and model risk—into a **living, real-time, sensing, learning system**.

We use the **A–E Framework**:

THE A–E AI-NATIVE RISK OPERATING MODEL

A. Risk Sensing

B. Risk Prediction

C. Risk Decisions

D. Risk Execution

E. Risk Learning

(see Figure 18.1)

Figure 18.1 – The A–E AI-Native Risk Loop

```
+---------------------------+
| E: LEARNING               |
+---------------------------+
| D: EXECUTION              |
+---------------------------+
| C: DECISION               |
+---------------------------+
| B: PREDICTION             |
+---------------------------+
| A: SENSING                |
+---------------------------+
```

We will now unpack each pillar across the **full risk universe**:

- Credit Risk
- Liquidity Risk
- Market Risk
- Fraud Risk
- Operational Risk
- Conduct and Behavioural Risk
- Compliance and AML Risk
- Model Risk
- Cyber Risk

You will receive a complete transformation blueprint—the definitive chapter on AI-first risk management.

1. WHY THE TRADITIONAL RISK MODEL FAILS IN THE AI ERA

Banks today face:

- real-time payments
- instant credit decisions

- hyper-connected supply chains
- behavioural fraud rings
- geopolitical volatility
- digital-only asset flows
- API-driven ecosystems

Traditional risk frameworks cannot respond fast enough.

1.1 The Five Structural Gaps of Legacy Risk

Gap 1 – Data Lag

Risk reports use stale data (weeks/months old).

Gap 2 – Human Bottlenecks

Escalations, approvals, committees slow everything down.

Gap 3 – Periodic Monitoring

Risk is reviewed monthly or quarterly—not continuously.

Gap 4 – Static Models

Scorecards and VaR do not adjust automatically to market shifts.

Gap 5 – Siloed Functions

Fraud, credit, AML, ops risk, market risk all operate separately.

1.2 AI Makes This Obsolete

AI-first risk systems:

- sense signals continuously
- connect all risk domains
- predict failures before they occur
- execute mitigations automatically
- learn from every event

Risk becomes **an intelligent mesh**, not separate departments.

(see Figure 18.2)

Figure 18.2 – Traditional vs AI-Native Risk

TRADITIONAL RISK:	AI-NATIVE RISK:
Periodic	Continuous
Siloed	Connected
Human-led	AI-augmented
Reactive	Predictive
Backward-looking	Forward-looking

2. A: RISK SENSING

Real-Time Data Collection Across the Full Risk Universe**

Risk sensing is the new frontline.

AI-native banks build systems that continuously capture signals from:

- transactions
- cashflows
- devices
- networks
- markets
- macroeconomics
- customer behaviour
- supply chain events
- geolocation
- interactions
- biometrics
- portfolio flows
- model performance

Risk sensing is the **radar** of the bank.

2.1 Risk Sensing Across All Risk Types

Credit Risk

Signals include:

- cashflow volatility
- income trends
- drop in salary consistency
- increased overdraft usage
- merchant-category changes
- abnormal repayment behaviour

Liquidity Risk

Signals include:

- deposit outflows
- funding concentration
- early-warning liquidity ratios
- market stress indicators
- intraday liquidity movements

Market Risk

Signals include:

- interest-rate fluctuations
- FX volatility
- yield curve movements
- commodity shocks
- geopolitical events

Fraud Risk

Signals include:

- device anomalies
- behavioural inconsistencies
- velocity attacks
- merchant-pattern deviation
- mules and rings

Operational Risk

Signals include:

- system health metrics
- batch delays
- failed payments
- staff behavioural anomalies

Conduct Risk

Signals include:

- call centre sentiment
- RM conversation patterns
- deviation from scripts

Compliance and AML Risk

Signals include:

- transaction graph movements
- counterparty risk changes
- unusual flows
- jurisdiction shifts

Cyber Risk

Signals include:

- abnormal network patterns
- unusual access behaviours
- deepfake voice or video attacks

2.2 The Real-Time Risk Sensing Mesh

All signals feed into a unified sensory fabric.

(see Figure 18.3)

Figure 18.3 – Risk Sensing Mesh

```
CUSTOMER DATA ----\
TRANSACTIONS -------> AI SENSING LAYER --> Risk Graph
MARKET DATA --------/
BEHAVIOUR ---------/
DEVICE-------------/
SUPPLY CHAIN ------/
```

Risk sensing is the foundation.

Once you sense, you can predict.

3. B: RISK PREDICTION

Using AI to Forecast Risk Before It Materialises

Prediction is the new backbone of modern banking risk.

AI models evaluate:

- probability of default
- fraud likelihood
- AML suspicion probability
- liquidity stress probability

- market exposure risk
- operational incident probability
- conduct risk anomaly

Risk prediction transforms risk management from:

- detecting events → anticipating them
- reacting → preventing
- monitoring → forecasting

3.1 Prediction Models Across Risk Types

Credit Risk Prediction

Models predict:

- PD (Probability of Default)
- LGD (Loss Given Default)
- EAD (Exposure at Default)
- forward-looking cashflows
- repayment patterns

Liquidity Risk Prediction

Models predict:

- intraday liquidity
- funding gaps
- deposit volatility
- stress conditions

Market Risk Prediction

Models predict:

- rate shocks

- FX volatility
- scenario impacts
- portfolio drawdowns

Fraud Prediction

Models detect:

- mules
- rings
- behavioural anomalies
- network links

AML Prediction

Models use:

- graph intelligence
- entity linking
- risk propagation

Operational Risk Prediction

Models detect:

- system failures
- workflow breakpoints
- human error patterns

Cyber Risk Prediction

Models detect:

- intrusion likelihood
- phishing probability
- compromised credential risk

3.2 Predictive Risk Graph

All predictions feed into a unified risk graph.

(see Figure 18.4)

Figure 18.4 – Predictive Risk Graph

```
    [Credit Risk Node]
            |
[Fraud Node]—+—[AML Node]
            |
     [Liquidity Node]
            |
     [Market Risk Node]
            |
   [Operational Risk Node]
```

Prediction sets the stage for decisions.

4. C: RISK DECISIONS

AI-Assisted Decisioning Across the Risk Universe**

Once the system predicts risk, the bank must **decide**.

An AI-native bank makes risk decisions:

- in milliseconds
- with full context
- with complete behavioural insight
- with explainability

Risk decisions include:

- declining a transaction
- adjusting a credit limit
- blocking a device
- triggering liquidity actions

- hedging a position
- raising collateral requirements
- escalating an AML alert
- initiating a fraud investigation
- adjusting operational workflows

4.1 Decision Engine for Risk Types

Credit Risk Decisions

- real-time approvals
- dynamic limits
- predictive restructuring
- adaptive pricing

Liquidity Decisions

- automated funding optimisation
- stress-driven collateral calls

Market Risk Decisions

- automated hedging
- exposure reduction
- risk rebalancing

Fraud Decisions

- block
- challenge
- step-up authentication
- behavioural verification

AML Decisions

- auto-classify
- escalate
- request documentation
- freeze account

Operational Risk Decisions

- reroute workflows
- trigger backups
- auto-recover systems

Conduct Decisions

- flag RMs
- enforce guidance
- trigger coaching

Cyber Decisions

- isolate systems
- block access
- auto-verify

4.2 The Risk Decision Engine

(see Figure 18.5)

Figure 18.5 – Risk Decision Pipeline

Prediction --> Explainability --> Policy Check --> Action Option --> Decision

Risk decisions are nothing without execution.

5. D: RISK EXECUTION

Taking Automated, Controlled, Real-Time Risk Actions**

Risk execution is how the bank carries out decisions.

Risk execution must be:

- fast
- accurate
- compliant
- monitored
- controlled
- reversible

5.1 Execution Across the Full Risk Universe

Credit Execution

- update limits
- modify pricing
- restructure loans
- schedule repayments

Liquidity Execution

- drawdown lines
- move liquidity
- rebalance buffers

Market Execution

- place hedges
- adjust positions
- reduce exposure

Fraud Execution

- block account
- issue step-up authentication
- freeze card

AML Execution

- file SAR
- freeze accounts
- notify regulator

Operational Execution

- route tasks
- rerun jobs
- alert teams

Cyber Execution

- isolate network
- block IP
- reset sessions

5.2 The Real-Time Risk Execution Fabric

(see Figure 18.6)

Figure 18.6 – Risk Execution Fabric

DECISION → ACTION → CONFIRMATION → LOGS → GOVERNANCE

Execution alone is not enough.

AI-native banks must learn.

6. E: RISK LEARNING

Continuous Feedback and Self-Improving Risk Models

Risk Learning is the pillar that makes AI-native risk **alive**.

Traditional risk learns:

- annually
- at model review cycles
- through post-mortems

AI-native risk learns:

- daily
- instantly
- through automated feedback
- through behavioural tracing

6.1 Feedback Sources

AI learns from:

- fraud outcomes
- default timelines
- repayment patterns
- device anomalies
- market reactions
- liquidity flows
- AML investigations
- cyber events
- operational failures

6.2 Model Learning Loop

(see Figure 18.7)

Figure 18.7 – Risk Learning Loop

Outcome → Evaluation → Drift Detection → Retraining → Deployment

6.3 Risk Learning Across the Risk Universe

Credit

- PD recalibration
- segment migration
- behavioural clustering

Fraud

- instant fraud patterns
- new attack vectors
- anomaly categories

AML

- typology reinforcement
- network discovery
- entity-linking upgrades

Market

- volatility patterns
- sensitivity recalibration

Liquidity

- stress threshold learning

Operational

- failure prediction refinement

Cyber

- threat intelligence updates

7. THE AI-NATIVE RISK CONTROL TOWER

The A–E system is orchestrated through a **Risk Control Tower**, integrating:

- dashboards
- predictive alerts
- early-warning signals
- portfolio heatmaps
- behavioural anomalies
- fraud trends
- liquidity stress views
- market exposures
- compliance flags

(see Figure 18.8)

Figure 18.8 – The AI Risk Control Tower

SENSE | PREDICT | DECIDE | EXECUTE | LEARN
(across ALL risk types)

8. GOVERNANCE OF THE AI-NATIVE RISK FUNCTION

AI-native risk still requires strong oversight:

- Model Governance Committee
- Risk Appetite Framework 2.0
- AI Risk Office
- Explainability Standards

- Human-in-the-loop Boundaries
- Real-time escalations
- Scenario governance

This ensures AI never operates without supervision.

9. ENDGAME: THE SELF-PROTECTING FINANCIAL INSTITUTION

When A–E is fully implemented, the bank becomes:

A self-sensing, self-correcting, self-learning risk organism.

It can:

- spot danger early
- adjust portfolios
- modify behaviour
- block threats
- protect customers
- optimise liquidity
- weather volatility
- reduce losses
- enhance resilience

This is not a risk function.

This is **autonomous resilience**.

10. CONCLUSION

This chapter delivered the definitive blueprint of the **AI-native risk function**.

Risk is no longer:

- manual
- periodic

- disconnected
- backward-looking

Risk becomes:

- real time
- predictive
- interconnected
- autonomous
- intelligent

The A–E risk operating model is the transformation engine for the bank of the future.

Risk intelligence keeps the bank safe at machine speed. But safety is not the endgame. The AI-first bank must also optimise value at machine speed—converting signals into profitability, capital efficiency, and shareholder returns. In Chapter Nineteen, we shift from risk governance to value governance, introducing the AI-First CFO Stack: Finance, Profitability and Capital Intelligence.

"Risk is no longer monitored—it is sensed, predicted, and shaped in real time."

CHAPTER 19

AI-FIRST CFO STACK: Finance, Profitability and Capital Intelligence

"Revenue is generated from products. Value is created in capital allocation."

This chapter redefines the role of the CFO in an AI-first bank. Finance moves from retrospective reporting and budget control to real-time value optimisation and capital intelligence. By integrating behavioural analytics, predictive risk signals, liquidity data, and product intelligence into a unified CFO stack, the bank continuously optimises profitability, capital allocation, RWA efficiency, cost-to-income ratios, and shareholder returns. The AI-first CFO does not measure performance after the fact—it dynamically steers it.

Walk into a traditional finance department, and you will find spreadsheets, closing cycles, variance explanations, and budget reviews. The CFO reports on what happened last month.

Walk into an AI-first CFO stack, and you see something radically different: live ROE heatmaps, behavioural margin analytics, dynamic RWA reallocation engines, predictive cost models, FTP optimisation flows, and scenario simulations running continuously.

Finance is no longer an accounting function.

It becomes the value intelligence engine of the institution.

In the AI era, the CFO does not ask, "How did we perform?"

The CFO asks, "How should we reallocate capital today?"

1. Why the Traditional CFO Model Breaks in the AI Era

For decades, finance operated on five structural assumptions:

1. Periodic reporting is sufficient

1. Product-level P&L is adequate
2. Capital allocation is strategic and infrequent
3. FTP is static
4. Cost optimisation is reactive

These assumptions no longer hold.

AI-first banking creates:

- Real-time credit decisions
- Embedded ecosystem distribution
- Dynamic pricing
- Continuous risk recalibration
- Intraday liquidity shifts
- Behaviour-driven profitability

A monthly finance cycle cannot steer a real-time institution.

The traditional CFO function is:

- backward-looking
- document-heavy
- spreadsheet-driven
- siloed from risk and treasury
- detached from behavioural data

The AI-first CFO stack is:

- continuous
- predictive
- behaviour-aware
- capital-intelligent
- cross-functional
- optimisation-driven

2. The AI-First CFO Operating System

All AI-native finance sits within a structured intelligence architecture.

2. The AI-First CFO Operating System

All AI-native finance sits within a structured intelligence architecture.

Figure 19.1 – The AI-First CFO Stack

```
+-----------------------------------------------------+
| LAYER 5: VALUE STEERING & BOARD INTELLIGENCE        |
+-----------------------------------------------------+
| LAYER 4: CAPITAL & RWA OPTIMISATION ENGINE          |
+-----------------------------------------------------+
| LAYER 3: PROFITABILITY & BEHAVIOURAL ANALYTICS      |
+-----------------------------------------------------+
| LAYER 2: REAL-TIME FINANCIAL DATA MESH              |
+-----------------------------------------------------+
| LAYER 1: SOURCE SYSTEMS (CBS, Risk, Treasury)       |
+-----------------------------------------------------+
```

Each layer transforms how value is created.

3. Layer 1 – Source Systems: The Financial Nerve Endings

The CFO stack integrates:

- Core Banking (balances, flows, margins)
- Credit engines (PD, LGD, EAD)
- Treasury systems (FTP, liquidity usage)
- Risk systems (capital buffers, stress results)
- Fraud systems (loss events)
- Product engines (pricing dynamics)
- Ecosystem APIs (embedded revenue flows)

In legacy banks, these are siloed.

In AI-first banks, finance sees the full organism.

4. Layer 2 – Real-Time Financial Data Mesh

Traditional finance uses monthly snapshots.

AI-first finance ingests:

- Intraday revenue signals
- Behaviour-driven margin changes
- Capital consumption fluctuations
- Liquidity usage patterns
- Segment-level risk shifts
- Ecosystem LTV changes

The CFO stack operates on live signals.

Finance becomes a streaming intelligence system.

5. Layer 3 – Profitability and Behavioural Analytics

This is where finance becomes intelligent.

Traditional profitability measures:

- Product margin
- Segment revenue
- Cost allocation

AI-native profitability measures:

- Customer-level RAROC
- Ecosystem-level LTV
- Behaviour-adjusted margin
- Capital-weighted return
- Liquidity-cost adjusted profitability

5.1 Behaviour-Adjusted Profitability

AI evaluates:

- Cashflow volatility
- Risk migration patterns
- Early delinquency signals
- Usage frequency
- Cross-sell probability

Profitability is dynamic, not static.

Figure 19.2 – Behaviour-Driven Profitability Loop

BEHAVIOUR → RISK SHIFT → CAPITAL USAGE → MARGIN CHANGE → ROE IMPACT

6. Layer 4 – Capital and RWA Optimisation Engine

Capital is no longer allocated annually.

It is dynamically steered.

AI integrates:

- PD / LGD / EAD
- Liquidity premiums
- Behavioural duration
- Funding costs
- Stress sensitivity

It then optimises:

- Risk-weighted assets (RWA)
- Capital buffers
- Growth allocation

- Portfolio composition
- Pricing strategy

6.1 Dynamic Capital Reallocation

Example:

If SME segment volatility rises →

Capital consumption increases →

RAROC declines →

AI recommends repricing or exposure adjustment.

Capital becomes fluid.

Figure 19.3 – AI Capital Intelligence Engine

RISK MODELS + LIQUIDITY DATA + BEHAVIOUR → CAPITAL CONSUMPTION MODEL

↓

OPTIMISE ALLOCATION

↓

ACTIONS

7. Layer 5 – Value Steering and Board Intelligence

At the top of the stack sits strategic value steering.

The AI-first CFO continuously optimises:

- ROE
- RAROC
- Cost-to-income ratio
- Capital buffer utilisation
- NII stability
- Risk-adjusted growth

Finance becomes a control tower.

Figure 19.4 – CFO Control Tower

ROE | RAROC | RWA | NII | COST RATIO | CAPITAL BUFFER

SEGMENT HEATMAP | ECOSYSTEM ROI | STRESS IMPACT | ACTIONS

8. Dynamic Pricing Linked to Capital

Traditional pricing ignores real capital cost.

AI pricing embeds:

- Risk premium
- Liquidity premium
- Capital charge
- Behavioural volatility
- Stress contribution

Pricing becomes capital-aware.

Product, risk, treasury, and finance operate on a unified logic.

9. Cost Intelligence and Operating Efficiency

AI-first cost optimisation includes:

- Process automation via LLMs
- Fraud loss reduction
- Operational risk prediction
- RM productivity analytics
- Workflow automation
- Smart resource allocation

Cost reduction becomes structural, not tactical.

10. Ecosystem Profitability in an Embedded World

The CFO stack tracks:

- Partner commission economics
- API monetisation margins
- Embedded credit yield
- Ecosystem-level LTV
- Platform-specific ROE

Finance must evolve from product economics to ecosystem economics.

11. AI-Driven Capital Planning and Scenario Intelligence

AI runs continuous:

- Growth simulations
- Rate shock scenarios
- Liquidity-capital interaction stress
- Portfolio rebalancing models
- Product launch capital impact analysis

Finance shifts from budgeting to scenario steering.

12. Integration With Risk and Treasury

An AI-first CFO does not operate in isolation.

It integrates:

Risk → capital consumption shifts

Treasury → liquidity premium signals

Credit → behavioural migration

Fraud → loss volatility

Distribution → ecosystem revenue

The CFO stack becomes the value integrator of the bank.

13. Governance of the AI-First CFO Stack

Intelligence must remain controlled.

Requires:

- AI Finance Oversight Committee
- Capital fairness review
- Explainable pricing protocols
- Stress governance framework
- Regulatory capital alignment
- Human override boundaries

Optimisation without governance becomes systemic risk.

14. The AI-Native CFO Profile

The AI-first CFO:

- understands models
- collaborates with CRO and CTO
- interprets behavioural data
- manages capital dynamically
- optimises risk-adjusted growth
- steers shareholder value continuously

Finance becomes strategic command—not reporting administration.

15. Endgame: The Autonomous Value Engine

When fully implemented:

The bank continuously:

- reallocates capital
- reprices products
- optimises segment mix
- reduces cost leakage
- increases risk-adjusted return
- balances growth and resilience

The balance sheet evolves from a static structure to an intelligent system.

16. Conclusion

In the AI-first bank, finance becomes the steering wheel—not the rear-view mirror.

Capital is no longer assigned annually.

It is orchestrated continuously.

Profitability is not reported after the quarter ends.

It is dynamically optimised in real time.

Value is not accidental.

It is engineered through intelligent allocation, behavioural insight, and disciplined governance.

If intelligence powers the bank...

If risk protects it...

If treasury stabilises it...

If finance optimises it...

Then one final question remains:

How does a CEO build all of this—deliberately, safely, and at scale—within 24 months?

That is where we turn next.

CHAPTER 20

From Vision to Execution: The CEO Playbook for Building an AI-First Bank in 24 Months

"In the end, banking does not become digital. Banking becomes intelligent."

This final chapter turns architecture into action.

It provides a disciplined, CEO-led execution playbook for transforming a digital bank into an AI-first institution—without destabilising the balance sheet, alienating regulators, or exhausting the organisation.

The 24-month window is the decisive period.

Within two years, a bank must move from scattered AI initiatives to a coherent, decision-centric operating model.

Full institutional maturity may take up to 36 months.

But by month 24, the transformation must be irreversible.

This is not a technology roadmap.

It is a leadership roadmap.

The bank will not win the future with the boldest AI slide deck.

The bank will win it with the clearest execution discipline.

You now have the full conceptual map:

how decision engines work

how AI reshapes risk, fraud, treasury, and finance

how intelligence becomes the operating system of the bank

What remains is execution.

Imagine a world where banks, fintechs, regulators, and AI systems form an interconnected intelligence network, detecting fraud across borders, reallocating liquidity in real time, pricing risk dynamically, and steering systemic stability autonomously. The future financial system behaves less like an industry and more like an intelligent organism. In this world, banking does not become more digital—it becomes fundamentally more intelligent.

"The bank does not win the future with the biggest vision.

The bank wins it with the clearest execution."

You now have the full conceptual map:

- what an AI-first bank is
- how decision engines work
- how AI reshapes risk, credit, fraud, AML
- how LLMs and agents transform operations
- how SME, treasuries, and platforms become intelligence-first
- what the 2030 endgame architecture looks like

But a strategy without execution is hallucination.

This chapter is a **playbook**.

Not theory.

Not philosophy.

A practical, structured, 24-month roadmap for CEOs, boards, and EXCOs who want to move from "digital bank" to **AI-first bank** while:

- protecting the balance sheet
- satisfying regulators
- carrying the organisation along
- avoiding hype-driven chaos

We'll go through:

1. A simple diagnostic: where are you today?
2. The three execution horizons (0–6, 6–18, 18–36 months)

3. The seven AI transformation workstreams
4. A 24-month AI execution roadmap
5. Metrics and dashboards for AI-first banking
6. Typical failure modes and how to avoid them
7. How to align the board, regulators, and investors
8. The final shift: from digital projects to an intelligence-first institution

1. Start Here: A Simple AI-First Readiness Diagnostic

Before you start building AI factories, launching copilots, or renaming teams, you need a brutally honest answer to one question:

"Are we a digital bank trying to add AI, or are we ready to become an AI-first bank?"

A quick, pragmatic diagnostic across **six dimensions**:

1. **Data**
2. **Technology**
3. **Risk and Governance**
4. **Products and Decisioning**
5. **People and Culture**
6. **Partnerships and Ecosystems**

Rate yourself on a 1–5 scale for each:

- **1** = Legacy, fragmented, manual
- **3** = Digitally capable, some analytics, pockets of AI
- **5** = AI-native, real-time, decision-centric

1.1 AI Readiness Heatmap

```
Dimension                Score (1–5)
----------------------------------
Data Infrastructure         __
Analytics / AI Stack        __
Risk & Model Gov            __
Products & CX               __
People & Skills             __
Partnerships / APIs         __
```

Your lowest 2–3 scores are **where your 24-month roadmap must start**, not where it is fashionable to start.

Many banks jump to:

- chatbots
- marketing use cases
- pilots in exotic areas

while ignoring:

- data foundations
- decision engines
- model governance

The AI-first bank is built **from the inside out**, not from the marketing layer down.

2. Three Execution Horizons: How AI Transformation Really Unfolds

To avoid "pilot theatre" and scattered efforts, you need a **time-structured play**.

We'll use **three horizons**:

1. **Horizon 1 (0–6 months)** – Foundations and Focus
2. **Horizon 2 (6–18 months)** – Scaling Decision Intelligence
3. **Horizon 3 (18–36 months)** – Full AI-First Operating Model

Think of it as a staircase, not a leap.

This playbook is designed for a 24-month CEO execution window. Horizon 3 extends to 36 months because full operating-model maturity takes longer, but by month 24, the transformation is irreversible.

2.1 The AI Execution Staircase

H3: AI-FIRST OPERATING MODEL (18–36m)
^
|
H2: DECISION INTELLIGENCE @ SCALE (6–18m)
^
|
H1: FOUNDATIONS & FOCUS (0–6m)

Each horizon delivers **tangible value**, not just architecture:

- H1: credibility and momentum
- H2: measurable financial impact
- H3: structural competitive advantage

3. The Seven Workstreams of AI-First Transformation

Across all horizons, the work is organised into **seven workstreams**:

1. **Strategy and Vision**
2. **Data and Intelligence Platform**
3. **Decision Engines and AI Models**
4. **Risk, Compliance and Governance**
5. **Products, CX and Journeys**
6. **People, Culture and Operating Model**
7. **Partnerships, Platforms and Ecosystems**

You do **not** need to move all seven at full speed on day one.

But you do need **all seven to be active** over 24–36 months.

3.1 AI Transformation Workstream Map

1. Strategy & Vision
2. Data & Intelligence Platform
3. Decision Engines & AI Models
4. Risk, Compliance & Governance
5. Products, CX & Journeys
6. People, Culture & Operating Model
7. Partnerships & Ecosystems

We'll now layer these workstreams onto the three horizons to create a concrete **24-month playbook.**

4. Horizon 1 (0–6 Months): Foundations, Focus and Proof

Objective:

Prove that AI can drive real value, while quietly building the minimal viable foundations.

Think of Horizon 1 as:

"Stop talking about AI. Show what it can do."

4.1 Strategy and Vision (H1)

- Form an **AI Strategy Council** chaired by the CEO or Deputy CEO.
- Define **3–5 "North Star" AI outcomes,** not 50 use cases.
  - e.g.: 30% faster credit decisions, 40% reduction in fraud false positives, 20% lower manual ops.
- Officially declare:

  "We are moving from digital transformation to intelligence transformation."

4.2 Data and Intelligence Platform (H1)

You don't need a perfect data lake in six months. You need:

- A **minimum viable data platform (MVDP)** that:
  - ingests core transaction data
  - exposes a **feature store** for 2–3 priority models
  - supports **online scoring** (not just batch reporting)
- Identify **data stewards** for key domains (customers, accounts, transactions, risk).

4.3 Decision Engines and AI Models (H1)

Pick **2–3 flagship decision areas** where AI can add visible value:

- retail credit decisioning for a specific segment
- fraud detection for cards or e-commerce
- SME working capital risk model
- collections prioritisation

Build:

- one **priority risk model** (e.g., behavioural PD)
- one **priority fraud model** (e.g., anomaly detection)
- one **simple decision engine** to orchestrate them

4.4 Risk, Compliance and Governance (H1)

- Establish a **Model Governance Committee (MGC)**.
- Create a simple **model inventory** (even if models are basic).
- Define:
  - approval process
  - monitoring thresholds

- documentation standards
- override policy

Regulators are more comfortable with **simple, documented AI** than with messy, opaque spreadsheets pretending to be "traditional."

4.5 Products, CX and Journeys (H1)

- Redesign **one journey** end-to-end with AI embedded:
  - e.g., SME overdraft journey
  - or retail top-up loan
  - or card fraud resolution
- Add:
  - dynamic decisioning
  - basic personalisation
  - LLM-generated customer communications

This proves AI doesn't just sit in risk analytics—it **touches customers**.

4.6 People, Culture and Operating Model (H1)

- Launch **AI Literacy 101** for EXCO, board, and top 200 leaders.
- Create **2–3 AI Product Pods**, cross-functional (product, risk, DS, tech).
- Appoint an **AI Transformation Leader** (not necessarily called "Chief AI Officer," but clearly accountable).

4.7 Partnerships and Ecosystems (H1)

- Decide:
  - build vs buy vs partner for key AI capabilities
  - which cloud / AI partners to shortlist

- Start **one structured external partnership**:
    - fraud/AML regtech
    - credit decisioning engine
    - or an LLM platform for internal pilots

4.8 Horizon 1 Summary Diagram

H1 (0–6M): FOUNDATIONS & PROOF

- AI Strategy Council formed
- 3–5 North Star outcomes
- Minimal viable data platform + feature store
- 2–3 flagship AI models in production (credit/fraud/collections)
- One AI-enhanced customer journey live
- Basic model governance in place
- AI literacy launched for leadership
- First key partner onboarded

If you end month 6 with this, you've already outpaced most of the industry.

5. Horizon 2 (6–18 Months): Scaling Decision Intelligence

Objective:

Move from isolated use cases to an **institution-wide decision engine**, with measurable P&L impact.

5.1 Strategy and Vision (H2)

- Translate vision into **portfolio-level AI OKRs**:
    - NPL reduction
    - fraud loss reduction

  - cost-to-income ratio improvement
  - CX metrics (NPS, resolution time)
- Identify **3–4 businesses/product lines** that will become "AI flagships":
  - e.g., SME, cards, personal loans, digital-only segments.

5.2 Data and Intelligence Platform (H2)

- Expand data platform to:
  - include **channel data** (app, web, branch logs)
  - integrate **CRM and collections data**
  - feed a **central feature store** consumed by multiple models
- Invest in:
  - streaming / real-time data
  - MLOps infrastructure for model deployment and monitoring

5.3 Decision Engines and AI Models (H2)

This is where **Decisioning-as-Core** truly begins.

- Design and implement a **central Decision Engine** that can:
  - orchestrate multiple models
  - run policy rules plus AI scores
  - support real-time and batch decisions
  - log decisions with explanations
- Expand from 2–3 models to a portfolio:
  - credit risk models across retail + SME
  - fraud models for cards, digital payments, and merchants
  - pricing elasticity models

  - churn prediction models
  - collections prioritisation models

5.4 Risk, Compliance and Governance (H2)

- Mature your **Model Risk Management Framework**:
  - risk tiering (high/medium/low impact models)
  - periodic independent validation
  - fairness/bias-testing requirements
  - clear retraining and decommissioning policies
- Introduce **AI Ethics and Responsible AI Charter**:
  - what you will not do, even if technically possible
  - how customers will be informed/protected

5.5 Products, CX and Journeys (H2)

- Expand from one journey to **a full cluster**:

  For example,
  - all unsecured lending journeys
  - all SME working capital products

Add:

- hyper-personalised offers
- dynamic limits
- predictive nudges
- AI-assisted customer support using LLMs
- proactive alerts (e.g. predicted cash shortfall offer restructuring)

5.6 People, Culture and Operating Model (H2)

- Expand **AI Product Pods** to cover:
  - Risk
  - CX
  - SME
  - Fraud and AML
  - Treasury (if advanced)
- Define an **AI Operating Rhythm**:
  - weekly model performance huddles
  - monthly decision-engine review
  - quarterly AI roadmap and value review
- Start shifting KPIs from:
  - "launch X projects"
  - to
  - "deliver Y improvement in decision quality/time/losses"

5.7 Partnerships and Ecosystems (H2)

- Launch **embedded finance or platform pilots**:
  - with fintechs, e-commerce, ride-hailing, logistics platforms
  - using your decision engine as the "brain"
- Establish:
  - standard API playbooks
  - risk-sharing frameworks
  - partner governance

5.8 Horizon 2 Summary Diagram

H2 (6–18M): DECISION INTELLIGENCE @ SCALE

- Central decision engine live
- 10–20+ models in production (credit, fraud, churn, pricing, collections)
- AI-enhanced journeys across a full product cluster
- Mature model governance & Responsible AI charter
- AI pods embedded into core businesses
- AI-driven partnerships / embedded finance pilots
- Clear, quantified financial impact visible in P&L

By month 18, AI is no longer a "project"—it is the **brain** of your core businesses.

6. Horizon 3 (18–36 Months): Full AI-First Operating Model

Objective:

Transform the bank into an **intelligence-first institution**, where AI is embedded in every meaningful decision, and the operating model, talent, and governance are fully aligned.

6.1 Strategy and Vision (H3)

- Explicitly reposition the bank as:
  - "An AI-first, decision-centric financial institution"
- Tie long-term strategy to:
  - model-driven capital allocation
  - intelligence-led risk appetite
  - AI-enhanced regional expansion
  - ecosystem plays

6.2 Data and Intelligence Platform (H3)

- Operate a **real-time data mesh**:
  - multi-domain
  - streaming-first
  - integrated with external signals (macro, open data, bureau, devices)
- Deploy:
  - multi-modal features (text, graph, behavioural, images where relevant)
  - online learning or frequent retraining cycles with strong governance

6.3 Decision Engines and AI Models (H3)

- Your decision engine now handles:
  - credit, fraud, AML, onboarding, pricing, collections, CX routing, treasury decisions
- Introduce:
  - **multi-agent systems** coordinating across risk, fraud, collections, retention
  - real-time experimentation (A/B testing of model strategies under policy guardrails)

6.4 Risk, Compliance and Governance (H3)

- AI risk becomes part of **enterprise risk management**, not a side topic.
- Regulators recognise you as:
  - a **trusted AI-led institution**
  - with transparent models
  - rigorous monitoring

  - collaborative supervision
- You may even help **shape national or regional AI banking standards**.

6.5 Products, CX and Journeys (H3)

- Products are fully **adaptive systems**:
  - dynamic pricing
  - continuous underwriting
  - self-optimising journeys
  - conversational frontends
- Customers experience your bank as:
  - proactive
  - protective
  - personalised
  - always-on adviser

6.6 People, Culture and Operating Model (H3)

- AI literacy is no longer optional; it is **standard** for all roles.
- Many roles become:
  - "human + AI co-piloted"
  - e.g. AI-augmented RM, AI-augmented underwriter, AI-augmented fraud investigator
- Organisation structure:
  - decision engines and AI platforms are as critical as core banking
  - model governance is part of everyday decision-making

6.7 Partnerships and Ecosystems (H3)

- The bank runs:

  - multiple large-scale embedded finance programmes
  - strategic partnerships across platforms, fintechs, regulators
- In many ecosystems, you are not just a participant—you are the **intelligence layer**.

6.8 Horizon 3 Summary Diagram

H3 (18–36M): AI-FIRST OPERATING MODEL

- Decision engine at the heart of the bank
- Intelligence layer serving all major business lines
- Products = adaptive, self-optimising systems
- AI embedded in risk, fraud, AML, CX, treasury, SME, platforms
- Workforce is AI-augmented, not AI-displaced
- Recognised by regulators as a safe, transparent AI-first institution

7. Metrics and Dashboards: How a CEO Should Track AI Transformation

You cannot manage what you cannot measure.

AI-first transformation requires **new KPIs**.

Think across **four layers**:

1. **Financial Impact**
2. **Decision Quality and Speed**
3. **Risk and Compliance**
4. **Adoption and Capability**

7.1 Financial Impact KPIs

- NPL ratio reduction (AI vs non-AI portfolios)
- fraud loss reduction vs baseline

- collections recovery uplift
- cost-to-income ratio trends
- revenue uplift from personalised pricing / cross-sell

7.2 Decision Quality and Speed

- average decision time (credit, onboarding, fraud resolution)
- % of decisions made by AI engines vs manual
- false positive/false negative trends in fraud, AML, risk
- override rates (how often humans overrule the model—and why)

7.3 Risk and Compliance

- number of models in each risk tier
- model drift alerts and resolution time
- fairness/bias metrics
- audit findings related to AI models
- regulatory feedback and remediation progress

7.4 Adoption and Capability

- of AI-augmented journeys live
- of active AI pods and use cases in production
- AI literacy % across role bands
- employee satisfaction with AI tools
- time to develop and deploy new models

7.5 Executive AI Dashboard (Conceptual)

```
+--------------- EXECUTIVE AI DASHBOARD ---------------+
| Financial Impact                                      |
|  • NPL Δ  • Fraud Δ  • Collections Δ  • CTI Δ         |
+-------------------------------------------------------+
| Decision Intelligence                                 |
|  • Decision time  • FP/FN errors  • Overrides         |
+-------------------------------------------------------+
| Risk & Governance                                     |
|  • Models by risk tier  • Drift alerts  • Fairness    |
+-------------------------------------------------------+
| Adoption & Capability                                 |
|  • AI journeys  • AI pods  • Literacy %               |
+-------------------------------------------------------+
```

8. The Failure Modes: How AI Transformations Derail

Most banks do not fail for lack of AI.

They fail for lack of **discipline and focus.**

Key failure patterns:

1. **Pilot Theatre**
    - Dozens of POCs
    - No scaled decisions
    - No P&L impact
2. **Tech-Only Transformation**
    - Cloud + tools + vendors
    - No operating model change
    - No cultural shift
3. **Model Without Governance**
    - Data scientists build clever models
    - Risk and compliance are bypassed
    - Regulator blocks progress

4. **Governance as a Brake, Not a Guardrail**
    - Every model takes 12–18 months to approve
    - AI becomes slower than manual processes
5. **No North Star, Just Noise**
    - No clear business outcomes
    - AI is everywhere in slides, nowhere in P&L
6. **Over-centralisation or Over-fragmentation**
    - Central AI team becomes a bottleneck
    - OR every business builds its own uncoordinated models

8.1 Avoiding the Pitfalls: A Simple Rule

"Balance ambition with discipline."

- Ambition = clear AI vision, strong executive sponsorship, 24–36 month roadmap.
- Discipline = governance, prioritisation, model risk management, value tracking.

9. Aligning the Board, Regulators and Investors

An AI-first transformation fails if:

- the board doesn't understand it
- regulators don't trust it
- investors don't see value

9.1 Board Alignment

- Run **board-level AI deep dives** focused on:
    - risk

- governance
- capital impact
- strategic positioning

- Give the board:
  - a clear view of AI-related risks
  - regular updates on models, incidents, and mitigations
  - transparent value tracking

9.2 Regulator Alignment

- Engage early and often:
  - share your AI roadmap
  - explain governance mechanisms
  - offer to pilot **supervisory sandboxes**
- Provide:
  - documentation
  - model cards
  - fairness metrics
  - incident reports

Regulators may start sceptical, but they respond well to:

- transparency
- humility
- structured governance

9.3 Investor Alignment

- Explain AI not as a buzzword, but as:
  - risk-adjusted growth engine

  - cost optimisation lever
  - competitive moat
- Share:
  - clear financial impact
  - AI-driven KPIs
  - strategic partnerships

10. From Projects to Institution: Making AI "How We Work"

The deepest shift is cultural:

AI stops being a project and becomes the way the bank thinks and operates.

That means:

- AI pods are part of business-as-usual
- Risk and model governance are integrated into normal decision flows
- Regulatory interactions assume AI is central, not peripheral
- Product teams design **with** models, not around them
- RMs, underwriters, and operations staff treat AI as copilots, not competitors

10.1 The AI-First Bank as a Living System

By the time your 24–36 month roadmap is in full stride, the bank behaves like a **living, intelligent system**:

SENSE → PREDICT → DECIDE → EXECUTE → LEARN

| | | | |

Data → Models → Decision → Processes → Feedback

- Every major decision is:
  - data-informed

    - model-supported
    - governed
    - monitored
- Every outcome:
    - feeds back into the system
    - improves future decisions

11. Closing the Loop: From Digital Transformation to Intelligence Transformation

Digital transformation:

- solved distribution
- improved UX
- automated workflows

But it stopped short of:

- changing how banks think
- re-architecting decisions
- making institutions adaptive

AI-first transformation:

- turns the bank into a **real-time decision engine**
- embeds intelligence in:
    - credit
    - fraud
    - AML
    - treasury
    - SME
    - CX
    - operations

The ultimate question for every CEO, board member, and regulator now is not:

"How digital is our bank?"

It is:

> **"How intelligent is our bank?"**
>
> **"How fast can we learn and adapt through AI?"**
>
> **"Are we building technology, or are we building institutional intelligence?"**

This playbook is your bridge between **vision and execution**.

The next steps are not about more reading—they are about decisions:

- picking the first 2–3 critical AI journeys
- designing your AI governance
- funding the data and decision engine
- building your AI pods
- aligning your board and regulators
- and committing, as leadership, to make intelligence the new core of your institution.

Because in the era ahead:

> **The bank with the best model**
>
> **and the clearest execution**
>
> **will win.**

"The intelligent economy doesn't wait for institutions to adapt—it rewards the ones that already have."

Banking will not disappear. But it will be reborn. The institutions that survive this decade will not be defined by their branches, their apps, or even their products. The quality of their decisions will define them—how quickly they sense change, how intelligently they predict risk, how precisely they allocate capital, and how responsibly they govern intelligence at scale. The AI-first bank is not a marketing label. It is a structural evolution from static institution to adaptive system, from periodic reporting to continuous learning, from manual judgement to model-augmented wisdom. The future will not belong to the biggest banks or the oldest banks. It will belong to the most intelligent ones. And intelligence, once embedded at the core, compounds.

Epilogue

Every era of banking has believed it was modern.

Until the next era arrived.

We are living through one of those moments.

Artificial intelligence will not politely sit alongside existing systems. It will reshape them. It will redefine credit. Reconfigure risk. Recalibrate capital. Redesign compliance. And quietly alter how trust is constructed in financial systems.

The question is not whether AI will transform banking.

It already is.

The real question is whether leaders will transform themselves fast enough to guide it.

The AI-First Bank demands more than technical capability. It demands courage. It demands boards that understand model risk as deeply as credit risk. It demands regulators who evolve from rule enforcers to systemic architects. It demands technologists who embed ethics into code before deployment.

This is not a story about replacing humans with machines.

It is a story about augmenting human judgement with intelligence—without surrendering responsibility.

Banking has always been built on trust.

In the age of AI, trust will no longer be derived from marble buildings or institutional longevity. It will be derived from transparency, explainability, and governance.

Those who embed intelligence responsibly will define the next century of finance.

Those who do not will fade quietly into infrastructure.

The age of digital banking made finance accessible.

The age of AI-First banking will make it aware.

The future of banking is not arriving.

It is being built right now by those bold enough to shape it.

Closing

Banking's future will not be defined by the intelligence we build, but by the responsibility we embed within it. For centuries, finance ran on trust in institutions; now it runs on trust in code. Yet code is never neutral; it carries the values of those who design it. As algorithms begin shaping opportunity, allocating capital, and influencing economic destiny, the true foundation of banking is no longer brick, branch, or balance sheet. It is judgement. It is governance. It is moral clarity. The institutions that endure will not be those that automated the fastest, but those that chose the wisest—understanding that when intelligence becomes infrastructure, responsibility becomes power.

**"When intelligence becomes the core of finance,
wisdom must become its conscience."**

www.ingramcontent.com/pod-product-compliance
Lightning Source LLC
LaVergne TN
LVHW090302210926
848480LV00001B/99
* 9 7 9 8 9 0 3 4 2 8 5 6 4 *